Riding the Windhorse

Spiritual Intelligence and the Growth of the Self

Kathleen D. Noble
University of Washington

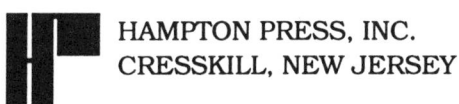

HAMPTON PRESS, INC.
CRESSKILL, NEW JERSEY

Printed in the United States of America

Library of Congress Cataloging-in-Publication Data

Noble, Kathleen Diane.
    Riding the windhorse : spiritual intelligence and growth of the
self / Kathleen D. Noble.
        p. cm.
    Includes bibliographical references (p.) and indexes.
    ISBN 1-57273-374-8
    1. Spiritual life. 2. Psychology, Religious. I. Title.

BL624 .N63 2001
291.4'2--dc21

                                                        2001024128

Cover illustration by Nicholas Kirsten Honshin

Hampton Press, Inc.
23 Broadway
Cresskill, NJ 07626

To those who shared their stories with me,
and to those who have stories to share

Contents

Acknowledgments

Writing a book is always like giving birth, but this one had an especially difficult labor and delivery. I am grateful to many friends and colleagues for their encouragement and careful reading of the manuscript at critical stages: Imants Baruss, Daniel Deslauriers, Don Hill, Susan Jeffords, Clark Johnson, Alexis Traynor-Kaplan, Todd Richards, Rose Robertson, Nancy Robinson, Elizabeth Rutledge, Mehmet Sarikaya, Nancy Sisko, and Jule Stein. I am particularly thankful to Norman Garmezy, Professor Emeritus at the University of Minnesota, for encouraging my interest in spirituality and resilience at a critical point in my career, and to the brave individuals who gave me access to their wisdom and their lives. Finally, I am indebted to Elizabeth Jenkins, Barbara Kerr, and Felicia Eth, councilors extraordinaire, who helped me keep the dream alive from beginning to end.

Prologue

*If you bring forth that which is within you, what you bring forth
will save you. If you do not bring forth that which is within you,
what you do not bring forth will destroy you.*
  —The Gnostic Gospels

I have long been intrigued by the interplay of spiritual and physical realities. Many years ago, I was captivated by these words and I remain so to this day. The American psychologist William James once reflected that "Most of us can remember the strangely moving power of passages in certain poems read when we were young, irrational doorways as they were through which the mystery of fact, the wildness and the pang of life, stole into our hearts and thrilled them" (1902, p. 375). The sensations aroused in me by this passage were like long-forgotten memories, reminiscent of vivid dreams I had had as a much younger child. My mother's sadness and rage had permeated my childhood home, as did my parents' ongoing war with each other. I often lay in bed at night, too terrified by their fights to get to sleep, praying desperately for help. In one memorable dream, an angel showed

1

me how to sit very still, flip a mental switch, and pass through to a higher reality where I could experience peace. Was this just a child's attempt to tune out trauma by dissociating from physical reality? Perhaps. Yet I felt certain that I was being shown the underlying presence of the spiritual realm. Years later I would use a similar technique in meditation to explore the experiences and enigmas raised by my study of metaphysics, and to guide me when I was searching for new life directions.

It may be that my acute sensitivity to the pain that poisoned our family life made me more open to spirituality than I would otherwise have been. Genetics may also have played a role. Relatives spoke of ancestors who had, and used, the gift of *Sight*, and telepathy was common among my siblings. Whatever the reasons for my fascination with the unknown, the result was a strong, abiding interest in the ways in which physical and spiritual realities inform one another.

My high school years were happily spent at a progressive, Catholic, women's high school in the Northeast where spirituality was an important part of life. Appreciation for the diversity of religions and philosophies was strongly encouraged by the Sisters of St. Joseph, who founded the school, and holy days of other faiths were occasionally observed in order to foster tolerance and awareness. When my belief in Roman Catholicism collapsed at age 14, two extraordinary nuns taught me to cast a wider net for spiritual wisdom. My studies, which began under their tutelage with Christianity, Judaism, Buddhism, and existential philosophy, broadened over the years to include psychology, physics, anthropology, and metaphysics. I explored several eastern religions and meditation disciplines, and learned how dreams and inner senses could be used to navigate life's rougher waters.

This quest was not an academic exercise, but a matter of absolute survival. At the age of 19, my determination to be psychologically well led to an abrupt and permanent estrangement from my parents, and I was thrust into an adulthood for which I was completely unprepared. I had to survive without their emotional or practical support, and to cope with the rigors and responsibilities of independence long before I was ready. Had I not learned to turn within for guidance, I would not have survived. But the guardian angels of my childhood remained vigilant and steadfast. Following their advice in a series of dreams, I hitchhiked across the country and eventually settled in the Pacific Northwest (Noble, 1994). Surrounded by the water and wilderness of this new world, I embarked on my first serious relationship, worked my way through college, and began to pursue a legal career. Then, on a cold, blustery October day in 1975, a profound spiritual experience altered the course of my life forever.

In the months preceding this pivotal event, I had fallen into a serious depression. My life was in turmoil, and I had no idea how to fix it. My partner was emotionally abusive, and I knew I should leave him, but because he provided my only sense of family and security, I could not wrench myself free. Although I had been training for a legal career, an internship in a defense attorney's office had presented me with an excruciating ethical dilemma, and I doubted I could cope with this omnipresent reality in the life of a lawyer. Not only were my personal and professional lives in upheaval, but I had spent many months wrestling with three spiritual questions, the answers to which I had been unable to discern. Was there ever a time when consciousness was annihilated, a time when one's identity was extinguished forever? How did the universe work? Was life on planet Earth a meaningless jumble of haphazard events, or was there some greater design at play? And what was the point of it all? The combined weight of these stressors strained my psyche to the point of collapse. Until I could find some relief, I was stalled.

Mid-morning on that fateful October day, my heart started to race. My curiosity turned to alarm when, instead of lapsing into its normal pace, it showed no signs of slowing down. I had no idea what was happening to me and, anxious and afraid, I turned to my partner and told him I thought I was having a heart attack. He laughed at me and said, "it was all in my mind." Suddenly I realized that he was right, although not in the way that he meant. Everything was "all in the mind," as the mystics claimed, and I was about to find out how. Seconds later I started to die, although a part of me shrieked, "That's impossible! I'm only 25, I'm too young to die!" I was terrified by the suddenness of death, until a voice pierced my fear and reminded me of something I had read long ago; that death was our constant companion, always on the left shoulder. That reminder triggered an abrupt emotional shift, the terror of impending death replaced by a deep, calm acquiescence. I let go and allowed myself to die.

Once I accepted my death I felt a tremendous sense of excitement and relief, and then my heart just stopped. I watched my body fall to the ground and felt a twinge of sadness that I had not said good-bye to my partner, but the pull to leave was far stronger than the desire to remain. It seemed as if a door that had been there all along had suddenly been thrown wide open, and I turned and raced through it.

I found myself sprinting through the darkened tunnel many near-death survivors have described, bursting into a level of reality in which everything seemed to be dancing and changing in constant but orderly motion. I entered into this dance, observing and experiencing my "self" combining and recombining in a seemingly infinite number and variety of forms. Some were organic, some inorganic; some were familiar while others were profoundly unfamiliar, at least in human terms. Sometimes I found myself occupying infinitesimally small particulate substances and then rapidly expanding to form a great gestalt. At the height of this experience I realized with a shock that I had no form at all. Yet all the while I continued to exist and to know myself, regardless of the form, or lack thereof, in which I found myself. Amid the zany exhilaration of this roller-coaster ride through the possibilities of consciousness, I perceived that this experience was designed to answer the first of my three conundrums. There was, it seemed, no point at which I did not know who "I" was; identity was absolute, infinite, and unbounded, much to my considerable relief.

With this realization I was whisked back into my body, which my partner, skilled in emergency medical procedures, had carried to our bed and was laboring to revive. Rather than feeling grateful for his ministrations, however, I was angry, upset, and in considerable pain. I did not want to be "back," and I was determined not to stay. Mentally, I turned around and left again, once more rushing through the passageway I had discovered on my first excursion into the realms of death.

This time I was drawn toward a new and very different level of reality and into what seemed like a large classroom, where a professorial-looking being awaited my arrival. As I placed myself beside her (him?) she looked at me with extraordinary empathy and laughter in her eyes and asked me what it was that I wished to know. "I want to know everything," I said, feeling as though I had been waiting a lifetime to say this precise thought to someone who might actually know. "I want to know how it all works." "Is that all?" she laughed. "Then watch."

The ceiling disappeared, becoming instead an enormous blackboard on which were written long and complex equations, which inexplicably made perfect sense. Each symbol contained vast yet precise amounts of information that I was invited to study, touch, and explore at my leisure. Every time I asked my guide for clarification of some concept or point, the symbols would swirl and rearrange themselves, not ceasing until I reached a measure of comprehension. Although most of the particulars are beyond my ability to translate, the essence of this experience remains as clear today as it was over 20 years ago. The vision of the universe I perceived was neither random nor predetermined but rather a vast and intricately organized community in which everything belonged and into which everything fit with the precision of a Swiss clock. Any change that occurred anywhere in the whole rippled simultaneously throughout its many parts and was immediately absorbed into a seamless harmony encompassed by a vast and loving intelligence. It seemed as if I stayed in this classroom for a very long time, asking as many questions as I wished, the answers limited only by my ability to formulate questions. At length I could think of no more and sat back, awestruck by the magnificence of the infrastructure I had beheld. My guide smiled, asked if I was satisfied, and when I sighed my assent returned me forthwith to my familiar body in the material world.

Despite what seemed like hours in an out-of-body state, only minutes had elapsed in the physical world. Although my partner strove to keep me alive, I was no more ready to be reinstated in this reality than I had been before. As I opened my eyes and watched him care for me, I was overwhelmed with feelings of love and appreciation for our relationship and a deep puzzlement as to why we had come together, given our irreconcilable and rancorous differences. Looking into his eyes I found myself peering down a long corridor of shared lifetimes, and I laughed when I realized that we were indeed very old and committed friends who had come together to "polish" each others' rough edges as only equally strong substances could do. With this discovery I felt that my life had completed its course. Having no further desire to stay and a longing to return to the peace and expanded awareness I had just encountered, I touched his face and asked him, please, to stop and let me go, a wish with which he complied. This final leave-taking was soft and exquisitely gentle, no longer impelled by impatience but rather more like the strains of a slow farewell. My consciousness floated leisurely upward, past the roof of our home, through the trees, hovering for a moment to marvel over the jewel-like park that is the planet Earth. Then with a last and loving look I turned, took wing, and headed home.

After a journey of dizzying speed I found myself in what seemed like the very center of the universe, a multidimensional vortex comprising an infinite number of intact realities all spinning and pulsating simultaneously. It was the only time during this spiritual event when I felt afraid and disoriented, surrounded by an infinity I could not grasp and in which I felt utterly lost, bereft of any sense of belonging to any one place. I was out of my depth, and I knew it. But just when my terror seemed at its height, I was suffused with feelings of safety and love and found myself cradled in the "hands" of a vast presence. Looking up, I gazed into an eye of incomprehensible awareness out of which flowed a tear of deep compassion for me, conveying not only acceptance but a complete understanding of why I had arrived so precipitously on its doorstep. I had never felt such love in all my life, and I knew, somehow, that I was looking into the heart of the universe, and, inexplicably, into the heart of my self.

With this realization, I was slowly carried up and into the eye, materializing in the midst of a group of several immense beings. They laughed as I flopped into place, one of them saying gently and with a total lack of judgment in its voice, "We tried to tell you before you left that you were taking on too much, but you never listen to anyone. You're such an impatient soul." With a delicate shake of a gossamer finger another continued, "Fortunately you did what you set out to do, but it was certainly touch and go at times." Ruefully, I had to admit they were right and that perhaps I had finally learned to pace myself. But what, I asked, was going on in our corner of the universe? I couldn't remember, and the state of the planet seemed far worse than anyone could have anticipated. "Watch," they said, and what unfolded before me was an extraordinary lesson in the history of our species.

It seemed as though we, as a collective consciousness, had been engaged in a crucial experiment for a very long time, attempting to synthesize and harmonize two vast and seemingly dichotomous concepts, one akin to what we call power, the other to what we call ethics or morality. Somehow we had selected the metaphor of duality as a core component of our physical experience, a kind of "secret code" that enabled us to work continuously on the problem even when we were unaware of doing so. Although the result of this experiment was not foreordained, I had a strong sense that we would accomplish our goal, not only because we were capable of doing so, but because the completion was necessary to a much larger design unfolding in the universal scheme of things. It was an awesome challenge in which everyone had a vital part to play whether she or he was consciously aware of it or not.

All journeys come to an end. As I sat back gazing in wonder at my ancient companions, they asked whether I wanted to remain where I was or return to my physical life. There was no compulsion, no pressure to decide one way or the other, though they were quick to say that I had completed the personal goals that had brought me to that life and I was free to choose a different adventure in consciousness. As I pondered what I had learned on my journey I realized that my life had indeed been born of a desire for growth, a growth I had determined could be most efficiently accomplished under conditions of adversity and pain. The higher purpose served by this choice was joy, the joy of being in physical reality, the joy of breaking free of old patterns, the joy of discovering inner resources I might never otherwise have cultivated, and the joy of acquiring a quality of self-knowledge I could achieve nowhere else. And I was reminded that we are never truly alone. Not only does there exist an immense network of intelligent and loving allies who sustain and support us as we struggle to grow, but also some portion of our larger self always comprehends what we are doing and where we are heading. No matter where we might find ourselves in the vast complexity of the whole, there is always a level of awareness that is old enough and smart enough to understand. And I was shown that each of us, no matter how small or insignificant we might sometimes feel, is vital to the whole, to a depth and degree we are wont to forget.

Did I want to stay or go back, they asked again. The choice was mine and mine alone, but I had to decide quickly, as one could be out of the body for only a brief amount of time before it would be too late to return. No words can capture the excruciating difficulty of this decision. I was quite happy wherever I was, deeply at rest and at home, yet I felt a tremendous curiosity and desire to be involved in the momentous changes I perceived were occurring in our sector of the cosmos. I knew that my life would never be the same and that in some ways it might even be more difficult than it had been before. But curiosity overcame my desire for a vacation. Three times I was asked, and three times I affirmed my decision to return, and after the third I was swiftly restored to my body, the doors to that ineffable realm locking irreversibly behind me. I opened my eyes, burst into tears, and promptly fell asleep.

It has been more than 20 years since I returned to my physical body, and in that time I have had my full share of the joys, surprises, tragedies, and disappointments that this life has to offer. Yet that experience crystallized my desire to understand the relationship among spiritual experiences, spiritual intelligence, and psychological growth. This book is the result of that journey.

CHAPTER ONE

The Enigma of Spirituality

I sent my Soul through the Invisible
Some Letter of that After-Life to spell
And by and by my Soul return'ed to me
And anser'd "I myself am Heav'n and Hell.
— The Rubaiyat of Omar Khayyam

What is spirituality? What kinds of experiences are considered to be spiritual? What does it mean to be spiritual? The answers to these questions depend on a number of factors, foremost of which is one's interpretation of the word "spirituality." Gregory Zilboorg (1941), an historian of medicine, warned that "(l)anguage, the most powerful expression of the human mind, is at the same time its weakest tool; words are steeped in the traditions of man's psychological development. New concepts and new knowledge are not infrequently ahead of the word" (p. 295). This is especially true in the spiritual realm.

Many different words have been used throughout the centuries to convey ideas about spirituality, and all religions and religious traditions have unique vocabularies for depicting what may be identical experiences. Yinger (1957) argued that "any definition of religion is likely to be satisfactory only to its author" (p. 18). The same could be said for spirituality. Some people equate spirituality with the beliefs and practices of an organized religion or with the experience of ultimate reality and use words like *God, Great Spirit, Creator*, or *Allah*. Others prefer secular terms like *Cosmic Consciousness*, the *Universe*, or *All That Is* that include a wider range of paranormal phenomena. My favorite term derives from the work of Buddhist philosopher Chogyam Trungpa (1985), who depicted spirituality as the *Windhorse*, or the energy of basic goodness that comes from nowhere but is always there. Regardless of what words one uses or how broad or narrow one's definition is, one can speak about spirituality only metaphorically, a factor that makes conversation across intellectual and philosophical borders extraordinarily difficult.

This factor is particularly problematic when psychologists attempt to study spiritual phenomena. Abraham Maslow, one of the first psychologists to explore spiritual experiences, called them *peak* and *plateau* rather than religious because he found that they often challenged the dogma that was taught in the traditional religion of the experiencer. Religion, Maslow argued, could and often did serve an individual or an institution as a defense against "the shaking experiences of transcendence" or spirituality (1970, p. 33). Other psychologists, like Robert Emmons, might disagree. For Emmons, "religion is a broader concept than spirituality, since religion may involve more than a search for the sacred. Religion may, for example, be a route toward intimacy, meaning, status, comfort, or a variety of other end-states" (1999, p. 94). I believe that spirituality is a broader concept than religion because it allows for experiences that are neither religious nor sacred but are routes for exploring the metapsychological and metaphysical dimensions of being. These differences of opinion mirror the ancient Sufi tale about the blind wise men who tried to describe an elephant by feeling only its trunk or its tail. Like the Sufi wise men, we can discuss only those aspects of spirituality that are within our conceptual reach. Even then, our values and beliefs, attitudes and ethics, cultural and religious reference points, and our own spiritual experiences define the limits of our understanding.

How common are spiritual experiences? No one knows for certain, but clearly they are not limited to any particular time or population. Rather, individuals have reported them with remarkable consistency from the widest possible variety of places, eras, and personal backgrounds. Demographic characteristics such as age, gender, race, socioeconomic status, education, and occupation appear to have little, if any, influence on their incidence and prevalence (Noble, 1987). Females are somewhat more likely than males to talk about their spiritual experiences, but that may be because society grants them greater permission to discuss their inner lives. Children are more likely to spontaneously report these experiences if the adults in their lives are comfortable hearing about them. Adults often describe spiritual phenomena that occurred in childhood with far more clarity than those they experience later in life, perhaps because their younger selves had not yet learned to suppress them.

A growing number of empirical instruments are available with which to study the incidence of spiritual experiences (e.g., Baruss & Moore, 1992; Friedman & MacDonald, 1997; Hood, 1975; MacDonald, 1997; MacDonald, Le Clair, Holland, Alter, & Friedman, 1995; MacDonald, Tsagarakis, & Holland, 1994), and numerous studies suggest that significant numbers of people have had what they consider to be a spiritual experience. For example, Andrew Greeley (1994) conducted a national survey of 1,467 people in 1973 and found that 35% reported having had an intense experience of union with a powerful spiritual force that seemed to lift them out of themselves. Fourteen years later he readministered his original questions to a new representative sample of 1,473 individuals and found that there had been surprising increases in all categories of spiritual experiences surveyed, a finding he attributed to the growing popularization of the subject by the mass media (Greeley, 1987).

Extending Greeley's earlier research to their own country, British researchers David Hay and Ann Morisy (1978) discovered that ecstatic, paranormal, or religious experiences were as widespread in the United Kingdom as they were in the United States. Thirty-six percent of the adults in their national survey of 1,865 people described being aware of or influenced by a power that was markedly different from their everyday selves. Carol Keutzer (1978) conducted a similar study with 146 college students in

Oregon and found that 65% reported that they, too, had once felt close to a "powerful, spiritual force." Thirty-four percent of the 305 persons interviewed by L. Eugene Thomas and Pamela Cooper (1980) recalled an intense spiritual experience, as did 88% of the 1,000 San Francisco Bay Area residents randomly surveyed by Robert Wuthnow (1978). Allman, De La Rocha, Elkins, and Weathers (1992) surveyed members of the American Psychological Association and found that 325 psychologists in full-time private practice reported having had at least one mystical experience in their lives. I think it likely that the vast majority of people have had encounters with the spiritual realm, although many are loath to discuss them for reasons that I discuss in Chapter Two.

What produces these experiences? Anything and everything, according to the literature. Spiritual events arise in a variety of ways and contexts and often stem from the ordinary events of daily life. They can occur in dream states and reveries, or result from listening to music, being in nature, attending religious services, or contemplating a work of art. A number of "trigger" situations have been identified, which include physical exercise, fasting, moments of quiet reflection, sensory isolation or overload, extreme fatigue, and sexual relations. Perhaps the most frequently reported catalyst is the survival of clinical death (Greyson & Stevenson, 1980; Klass & Gordon, 1978; Noyes & Slymen, 1979; Ring, 1980, 1984; Sabom, 1982), a phenomenon that has been experienced by at least 8 million adults in the United States alone (Ring, 1984).

Numerous meditative disciplines have developed over the centuries (such as Sahaja, Zazen, Sufism, Yoga, and contemplative prayer) that have as their principal objective growth in spiritual awareness. The practice of meditation dates from ancient times and is found in one form or another in every system of worship (Goleman, 1976; Le Shan, 1974, 1976; Shapiro, 1980; Underhill, 1911). Not surprisingly, each style of meditative practice has its specific vocabulary, breathing and focusing technique, and amount of physical activity. Some forms involve dancing; others involve rhythmic breathing and precise body postures. Some require the eyes to be open; others require the eyes to be closed. Some advocate sitting in a particular position and chanting a mantra or prayer; others teach people to watch their thoughts and feelings and learn to let them go. New technologies developed by Western scientists and engineers use synchronized sound and light patterns to help people achieve deep states of relaxation, concentration, and spiritual awareness (Monroe, 1977, 1985).

Once confined to monasteries and ashrams, meditation is now widely taught in educational and medical settings, and to people of all ages and walks of life. The practice has produced a burgeoning scientific literature that documents its many physiological and psychological benefits (e.g., Bloomfield, 1980; Boorstein, 1980; Delmonte, 1980; Fling, Thomas, & Gallaher, 1981; Goleman, 1976; Hjelle, 1977; Shapiro, 1980; Spanos, Steggles, Rodtke-Bodorik, & Rivers, 1979). Meditation produces deep relaxation and increases concentration and self-awareness. It also relieves stress, decreases pain, and mitigates depression. It enhances an individual's ability to cope with challenging situations and strengthens feelings of self-confidence and self-worth, thereby promoting emotional integration. It also enables an individual to be receptive to phenomena that are often ignored in the waking state, such as dreams, intuitions, and psychic perceptions. Ultimately, however, meditation is designed to enable people to access their spiritual dimensions. "The mind settles down to a profound inner silence, a state of expanded awareness in which one recognizes one's innermost self as distinct from the roles, programs, and conditioning of one's external, more bounded existence" (Bloomfield, 1980, p. 134).

Although many meditation teachers claim that profound spiritual experiences are accessible only to great masters and adepts who have spent years in rigorous preparation, as is seen later in this book, this is not always the case. Some people meditate their entire lives without ever attaining the goal of enlightenment; others achieve that awareness within a short period of practice. And some have the awareness thrust on them without looking for it. This latter situation sometimes arises when people use consciousness-altering drugs.

The use of drugs to attain spiritual insights is a highly controversial subject. Many people are deeply disturbed by the idea that a chemical substance can trigger powerful spiritual events, and some Eastern, Western, and Native American religious leaders have condemned the use of hallucinatory substances to further a spiritual quest (McGaa, 1992). The complaint most frequently heard is that spiritual experiences attained in this way are not real because they are too easily achieved, "with the implication that they are unearned and therefore undeserved" (Pahnke, 1972, p. 257). Another argument is that "altered states achieved with drugs are distractions, inhibiting progress toward genuine enlightenment" (D. R. Hill, personal communication, April 28, 2000). Negative descriptions of people who use psychoactive drugs are common in contemporary psychiatric and psychological literature, and some scientists argue that spiritual experiences that arise from ingesting a drug are merely the result of complex brain chemistry. The personal and social havoc caused by illicit drug usage is so widespread that many people refuse to acknowledge the possibility that psychoactive drugs could produce any beneficial, spiritual effect. But because many people have had spiritual experiences as a result of drug experimentation, it is important to see this issue in its cultural and historical context.

In his classic study of drugs and higher consciousness, Andrew Weil, a physician and ethnobotanist, reported that "the use of drugs to alter consciousness . . . has been a feature of human life in all places on the earth and in all ages of history" (1972, p. 17). For example, in the sixth century BC, the body of sacred Zorastrian writings known as the Zend-Avesta recommended cannabis as an aid to meditation. The ancient Hindu text, the Rig Veda, also makes reference to the ritual use of the drug *soma*, which may have been derived from the mushroom, *Amanita muscaria*. Native peoples in the remote region of Huatha, Mexico used this same mushroom as an integral part of their sacred ceremonies for hundreds of years before their colonization by Spain. Although Catholic missionaries made great efforts to eradicate this practice, it continued to flourish in secret and to be used for healing, guidance, and other shamanic purposes. "The mushroom is held in great reverence, and anything uttered under its influence is believed implicitly to be the utterance of the gods themselves" (A. Puharich, 1974, p. 56). The use of a special mushroom was also believed by ancient Taoists to confer on the seeker visions of the immortality of the soul, and it was recommended in the *Tibetan Book of the Dead* to help dying persons achieve an easier transition from physical to spiritual reality.

Amanita muscaria continues to be used by the Koryak, Chukchi, and the Tungus peoples in northeastern Siberia "in order to have the travelling-soul experience" (p. 140), a practice that is considered to be one of the greatest feats of shamanism.

There is evidence that as early as 300 BC, the Aztecs used the dried heads of the peyote cactus (whose active ingredient is mescaline) for spiritual purposes. This same substance has been used as a sacrament in the pan-Indian Native America Church since its inception in the 1870s. Contemporary groups of South American Indians also use psychoactive drugs to enhance their spiritual awareness. Weil spent many years with indigenous peoples of Central and South America and learned that for these societies, unlike those in Western cultures, the use of consciousness-altering drugs had virtually no personal or communal ill effects. "Drug-induced states are not entered for negative reasons (such as escape from boredom or anxiety) because they can be of positive usefulness to the individuals and the tribe" (1972, p. 109). Rather, they are taken purposefully, in highly ritualized ceremonies, and under the guidance and supervision of a tribal elder.

In contemporary Western countries, psychoactive drugs gave many people their first inkling that consciousness was not limited to the waking state. As Weil observed about himself, "I and many of my friends would never have thought about meditation, higher levels of consciousness, or spiritual matters if we had not been in contact with the drug subculture and had been through phases of meaningful use of marijuana and hallucinogens" (p. 195). It was William James' experiment with nitrous oxide in the late nineteenth century that unlocked the doors of his perception and resulted in his classic study, *The Varieties of Religious Experience*. As a result of this experiment, James reached a conclusion that guided much of his life's work.

> It is that our normal waking consciousness, rational consciousness, as we call it, is but a special type of consciousness, whilst all about it, separated from it by the filmiest of screens, there lie potential forms of consciousness entirely different. We may go through life without suspecting their existence; but apply the requisite stimulus and at a touch they are there in all their completeness, definite types of mentality which probably somewhere have their field of application and adaptation. No account of the universe in its totality

can be final which leaves these other forms of consciousness quite disregarded. How to regard them is the question—for they are so discontinuous with ordinary consciousness. Yet they may determine attitudes though they cannot furnish formulas, and open a region though they fail to give a map. (1902, pp. 378-379)

What exactly *are* the experiences that people are labeling as "spiritual?" Not surprisingly, they are extremely diverse and subject to individual interpretation. Matthew Fox (1981), a Roman Catholic priest and creation theologist, might describe a spiritual experience as "our growth in ecstatic consciousness and our sharing of it. . . . Not a flight from creation but a recreation of the way we taste creation" (p. 238). A Zen master might offer the dream of a woman dreaming she is a butterfly dreaming she is a woman. For someone else, it might be a profound insight, an extrasensory perception, or a powerful dream. As Imants Baruss remarked, the experiences people identify as spiritual "range from experiences with some identifiably spiritual content to having had a good time at summer camp. . . . If anything counts as a spiritual experience then 'spiritual' doesn't characterize anything" (personal communication, September 1999). Baruss makes a valid point, one with which William James, a pioneer in the psychology of religion, would have agreed: "So many men, so many minds: I confess that these experiences can be as infinitely varied as are the idiosyncrasies of individuals" (1902, p. 339).

SO MANY EXPERIENCES

One group of experiences to which many people apply the label "spiritual" are those that involve contact between individuals and what they perceive to be the Supreme Being or ultimate reality. Reports of these kinds of experiences are ancient and universal, although, once again, different terms are used to describe them. The Hindu word *Yoga* literally means "union with Divine Reality." Buddhists use terms like *Samadhi* and *Satori*, Sufis speak of *Fana*, Taoists the *Tao*, and Catholics the *Beatific Vision.* Quakers use the phrase *Inner Light* to portray what Hasidic philosopher Martin Buber called *I-Thou*, and Don Juan, a

Yaqui Indian sorcerer, speaks of the *Nagual. Mystical experience* is a term used in many branches of Christianity, whereas transpersonal psychologists prefer *transcendent* or *peak experience*. Later in this book I describe such experiences as *crystallizing* to convey their impact on the psyche, but all these terms can be used interchangeably.

Like all spiritual events, these experiences arise in a variety of ways: contemplative practices such as meditation or prayer, ingesting a consciousness-altering substance, listening to music, creating or appreciating a work of art, and psychological need are but a few (James, 1902; Noble, 1987; Underhill, 1911). Their occurrence is spontaneous and unpredictable, and they can last anywhere from a few seconds to a few days. While they are transpiring, dimensions of time and space lose all meaning and relevance. Words like peace, happiness, wonder, awe, reverence, acceptance, compassion, and love are commonly used to convey their emotional impact, but the overriding sense is best described as *noetic joy*. One has an awareness of the perfection and sacredness of the universe, an acceptance of the rightness of one's being regardless of one's current life circumstances, and a certainty that all existence is meaningful and utterly interconnected.

One of the earliest accounts of this kind of spiritual experience was recorded by an orthodox Jew named Philo who lived in Alexandria approximately 2,000 years ago. Although little is known about him, his encounters with the "Sublime Abyss of the Unfathomable Wisdom" were to have a profound impact on the mystical canon of the developing Christian faith.

> Sometimes when I have come to my work empty, I have suddenly become full; ideas being in an invisible manner showered upon me, and implanted in me from on high; so that through the influence of divine inspiration, I have become greatly excited, and have known neither the place in which I was, nor those who were present, nor myself, nor what I was saying, nor what I was writing; for then I have been conscious of a richness of interpretation, an enjoyment of light, a most penetrating insight, a most manifest energy in all that was to be done; having such an effect on my mind as the clearest ocular demonstration would have on the eyes. (quoted in Underhill, 1911, p. 64)

Philo's most influential disciples were Plotinus, a third-century Neoplatonic philosopher, St. Augustine (354-430 CE), and Dionysius the Areopagnite (475-525 CE), the latter two becoming pillars of the Roman Catholic Church. "Through these three, there is hardly one in the long line of the European contemplatives whom his powerful spirit has failed to reach" (Underhill, 1911, p. 456).

Dionysius was a mystic and a scholar who employed the metaphor of angels to describe his spiritual insights and perceptions. He used the term *Seraph* to portray those angels "closest to God" who embodied perfect love and *Cherub* for those who symbolized perfect knowledge. For Dionysius, these twin images were inseparable and comprised the totality of supreme reality. In 850 CE, John Scotus Erigena, an Irish philosopher, theologian, and occasional member of the court of Charlemagne, translated Dionysius' insights from Greek to Latin. His translation "marked the beginning of a full tradition of mysticism in Western Europe" (Underhill, 1911, p. 457), one that gave rise to an explosion of monasteries and cloistered religious orders through which contemplative individuals could pursue their quests for spiritual truth.

The Catholic Church considered Hildegard of Bingen, a twelfth-century Benedictine abbess, a great prophet and mystic during her lifetime. She experienced ultimate reality as the Living Light "which was brighter than the brightness surrounding the sun" (Underhill, 1911, p. 64). Other Catholic mystics, such as St. Francis of Assisi and St. John of the Cross, described their spiritual awakenings in terms of *Divine Love*, and St. Teresa of Avila spoke of an "infused brightness, a light which knows no night; but rather, as it is always light, nothing ever disturbs it" (p. 249). The metaphor of light was also used by the fourteenth-century Italian poet Dante Allegiri, who wrote passionately and prolifically about the *Semplice Lume*, and by the nineteenth-century American poet, Walt Whitman, who extolled *Light, rare, untellable!*

Spiritual experiences of this magnitude are by no means confined to Christian mystics or poets. The Zohar, the Hindu Veda, and the Zoroastrian Zend-Avesta contain numerous descriptions of similar events. Indeed, some experiences of ultimate reality reported by Christian and Jewish mystics are remarkably similar to those found in Zen, Sufi, and Hindu litera-ture. Hindus, for example, recount the story of two notorious fig-ures, Jagai and Madhai ("on whom Sri Caitanya poured down his compassion so unexpectedly and in such abundance" [Basu, 1983, p. 16]), which predates but resembles the conversion of Saul/Paul on the road to Damascus. Sufism, the mystical branch of Islam, was the spiritual home of Al-Ghazzali, an eleventh-cen-tury philosopher and theologian. His autobiography includes an encounter with the Divine Light that is virtually identical to that of George Fox, who founded the Society of Friends in England some 600 years later (Fox, 1981).

Just as the visions of Moses, Jesus, Mohammed, and the Buddha are the cornerstones of the religious traditions that grew around them, so are new faiths built on the spiritual experiences of their founders. When Martin Luther overheard a fellow monk repeating the words "I believe in the forgiveness of sins," he had a profound revelation. "I saw the scriptures in an entirely new light; and straightaway I felt as if I were born anew. It was as if I had found the door of paradise thrown wide open" (Underhill, 1911, p. 373). Shortly thereafter, Luther's public protest against the excesses of the Roman Catholic Church ignited the Reformation, which made possible myriad new expressions of Christianity. George Fox's Society of Friends was one such group. Others included the Christian Science Church, founded by Mary Baker Eddy after her powerful experience of faith healing, and the Church of Jesus Christ of Latter Day Saints, inspired by Joseph Smith's encounter with the angel Moroni. In the mid-nineteenth century, the Persian prophet Bha'u'llah perceived a vision of the oneness of all religions and all prophets that laid the foundation for the international Bah'ai movement 100 years later.

Despite the best efforts of many people to describe the content and impact of these kinds of spiritual experiences, words remain hopelessly inadequate to the task. Every person who has had such an experience knows how painfully difficult it is to describe. Teilhard de Chardin, a priest, philosopher and eloquent mystic, lamented that "all that I shall ever write is only a feeble part of what I feel" (quoted in King, 1980, p. 24). Alfred Lord Tennyson, one of the greatest masters of the English language, was similarly frustrated by his inability to do justice to a pro-found experience he first had as a boy:

This has come upon me through repeating my own name to myself silently, till all at once, as it were out of the intensity of the consciousness of individuality, individuality itself seemed to dissolve and fade away into boundless being and this not a confused state but the clearest, the surest of the surest, utterly beyond words, where death was an almost laughable impossibility, the loss of personality (if so it were) seeming no extinction, but the only true life. I am ashamed of my feeble description. Have I not said the state is utterly beyond words? (quoted in James, 1902, pp. 374-375)

If Teilhard and Tennyson were at a loss for words, how much harder it is for those of us who do not share their verbal fluency.

Not all experiences that people consider to be spiritual are of the transcendent variety. Indeed, some are quite prosaic. Included in this group is extrasensory perception (ESP), a means of acquiring information via channels that are not known to be sensory in nature (Radin, 1997). ESP includes phenomena such as telepathy and clairvoyance (direct mind-to-mind communication) and remote viewing (Targ & Katra, 1998; Targ & Puthoff, 1977). Synchronicity, a word coined by Carl Jung to describe a meaningful coincidence, might also be a form of ESP. A synchronistic event is one in which everything one needs seems to fall into place and one feels connected to a larger, more purposeful whole. It can also have a somber side. Jung recalled an experience with a patient whom he had been treating for depression. The patient had failed to keep an appointment one day, and Jung was worried. He felt increasingly anxious as the day progressed and had considerable difficulty falling asleep that night.

At around two o'clock. . . . I awoke with a start, and had the feeling that someone had come into the room. . . . I instantly turned on the light, but here was nothing. . . . Then I tried to recall exactly what had happened, and it occurred to me that I had been awakened by a feeling of dull pain, as though something had struck my forehead and then the back of my skull. The following day I received a telegram saying that my patient had committed suicide. He had shot himself. Later I learned that the bullet had come to rest in the back wall of the skull. (1965, p. 138)

Altered states of consciousness are considered by many people to be spiritual events. These include a wide range of experiences that occur within dimensions of reality that seemingly lie beyond the waking state. They "appear to be ways to make more effective and fuller use of the nervous system, to the development of creative and intellectual faculties, and to the attainment of certain kinds of thought that have been deemed exalted by all who have experienced them" (Weil, 1972, p. 36). Different states of consciousness have been found to enhance coping skills, help resolve emotional conflicts, and augment various healing arts and practices (Asrani, 1972; Ludwig, 1969; Nash, 1976; H. Puharich, 1974; Simonton, 1978; Tart, 1969, 1975; White, 1972). Stanley Krippner (1972) differentiated 20 different states of consciousness, some of which enhance artistic and creative insights. Mozart, for example, while in a semi-trance, frequently heard entire musical compositions which he then proceeded to write down. Richard Bach said that much of his novel, *Jonathan Livingston Seagull*, was dictated to him in a dream. Mathematician John von Neumann had a well-known habit of thinking about problems as he went to sleep and then awakening in the middle of the night with an understanding of how to proceed. According to his colleague, Herman Goldstine, "He never seemed to wrestle with a difficulty as did some of his colleagues. Either it had to come elegantly and easily, or he put it aside until it suddenly did" (Arus, Davis, & Stuewer, 1983, p. 310). The nineteenth-century chemist Kekule discovered the structure of the benzene ring in a similar way. After years of determined but frustrated effort, he fell asleep one day and saw rows of atoms moving together in a serpentine fashion.

> And see! What was that? One of the serpents seized its own tail, and the form whirled mockingly before my eyes. I became awake, as though by a flash of lightning. This time I spent the remainder of the night working out the consequences of the hypothesis. If we learn to dream, gentlemen, then we shall perhaps find truth. (quoted in Bunge, 1962, pp. 83-84)

Another altered state is the out-of-body experience. The ancient Greeks had a tradition of men who could detach their souls from their bodies and travel to distant physical or spiritual lands to obtain information about a variety of subjects, including medical and military advice (H. Puharich, 1974). Similar accounts are found in the Zohar, a collection of stories that first appeared in the thirteenth century about the quests of prominent Jewish rabbis for personal enlightenment, knowledge of divine mysteries, protection of the community, and the coming of the Messiah. "These masters function[ed] as shamans, going into trances, communicating with angels and spirits of the dead, confronting evil spirits, and, in general, demonstrating their mastery of all the spiritual and physical realms" (Schwartz, 1993, p. 6). Stories about people with similar talent appear in the chronicles of medieval Western monasteries, in the legends of the Tohunga in New Zealand, and among the Koryak, Chukchi, and the Tungus peoples of Siberia. They are also reported by indigenous peoples of Central and South America and by practicing members of the Native American Church (A. Puharich, 1974).

Although generally considered one of the greatest feats of shamanship or sainthood, several studies indicate that with proper training—and often without—out-of-body experiences are potentially available to everyone. Edgar Cayce, a poorly educated man who lived in the rural American South during the early twentieth century, fell asleep one day and found that he could leave his physical body and retrieve accurate diagnostic information about numerous physical and psychological maladies from a spiritual place he called the Akashic Records (Johnson, 1998). Researchers at the Stanford Research Institute conducted remote-viewing experiments with a wide variety of participants and documented the ability of several subjects to gather uncannily accurate information from remote locations without leaving their physical bodies (Targ & Katra, 1998; Targ & Puthoff, 1977). Not all out-of-body travel occurs in what we consider to be present time. Robert Monroe was a skeptical engineer who lay down for a nap one afternoon and suddenly found himself conscious and "ambulatory" in noncorporeal space. His subsequent out-of-body experiences included several in the past and the future and in what he described as simultaneously occurring, alternate lives (Monroe, 1977, 1985).

Sightings of apparitions or spirit guides are relatively common events. The tradition of seeing nonphysical entities is universal and generally falls into two categories: the "good" dead (e.g., angels, spirit guides, deceased loved ones) and the "bad" dead (malevolent beings who wreck havoc in human lives). The Old and New Testaments of the Bible, the Zohar, ancient Egyptian papyri, and medieval French manuscripts, among other documents, describe spirits on both sides of the spectrum interacting with prophets, saints, and ordinary people.

Although Western scientists generally dismiss nonphysical entities as imaginary, Ian Stevenson, a psychiatrist and professor at the University of Virginia, found that "in Great Britain and the US, several surveys have shown between 10 and 17% of respondents from the general population *believe* they have seen at least one apparition" (Stevenson, 1987, p.19; emphasis in original). Stevenson spent more than 30 years conducting longitudinal and cross-cultural studies of young children who spontaneously recalled other lives, and he carefully documented their vivid accounts of where they had lived and with whom, as well as how they had died. He found that these children expressed definite preferences for certain foods that were not served in their current homes, and occasionally spoke a foreign language when recalling past life memories-often more fluently than their new tongue. Stevenson's subjects spoke less often of their former lives as they matured, and by the time they reached the age of seven, most were firmly ensconced in their new identities (1974, 1987). David Feldman (1986) reported the case of a child prodigy who, at the age of 18 months, was playing in his bath when suddenly his body went rigid and he began to scream in terror about "the men who were coming" (p. 194). These episodes repeated themselves over a period of about two years, accompanied by an increasingly detailed story of how he watched the Nazis murder his entire family in a previous life.

Reports of encounters with spiritual beings are well represented in the near-death experiences of children and adults (Morse, 1990, 1994; Ring, 1984) and are commonly perceived by those who are terminally ill or dying. Psychologists Karlis Osis and Erlendur Haraldsson (1977) conducted an extensive, cross-cultural study of more than 1,000 people who had visions of an afterlife shortly before their death. Most people reported the presence of a deceased parent, spouse, sibling, or friend who had come to help them cross the border between the worlds, but some apparitions appeared in guises that were completely unexpected. Two deceased Nobel Laureates visited a dying scientist who was firmly opposed to the idea of an afterlife, to help him deal with his terror of oblivion. A devout Christian encountered the Prophet Mohammed; the Virgin Mary comforted an orthodox Jew; Krishna greeted a dying Muslim.

> The phenomena within each culture often do not conform to *religious afterlife beliefs*. The patients see something new, unexpected, and contrary to their beliefs. Christian ideas of "judgement," "salvation," and "redemption" were not mirrored in the visions of our American patients. . . . Several basic Hindu ideas of an afterlife were never portrayed in the visions of Indian patients. (Osis & Haraldsson, 1977, p. 190; emphasis in original)

Clearly, the kinds of experiences that people call spiritual are extremely diverse and seemingly ubiquitous. Unfortunately, studies of their incidence, prevalence, and effects on people's lives are confounded by a number of factors, including the quantity and quality of questions that a researcher asks, the personality of the researcher, the criteria used by examiners to evaluate responses, people's understanding of these experiences, and their interpretation of the questions they are asked. Adding even more complexity to this situation is the psychological climate in which research about spirituality is conducted. As Greeley (1974) observed, "whether we notice [these experiences] or not is probably a function of whether they are at any given moment culturally acceptable" (p. 11).

CHAPTER TWO

Psychological Resistance to Spiritual Events

No new step is ever made and no new discovery is ever brought forth without the shadows of the past hovering over it.
—Gregory Zilboorg (1941)

There is a story, perhaps apocryphal, that I overheard when I was small. My Irish grandmother's elder sister had been blessed with the gift of *Sight*, and friends and neighbors often sought her advice. One day a priest, newly assigned to the parish, learned of this practice and forbade her under pain of excommunication to speak of such things. He believed that her ability was a manifestation of the devil. Because excommunication meant ostracism in rural Catholic villages of nineteenth-century Ireland, my great-aunt complied with the priest's demand. Three months later she suddenly and mysteriously died.

Why was this story whispered in our family? Although extrasensory perception was common among the children, it was a source of great uneasiness to the adults. As a very young child

I often saw colorful halos around people's heads, but when I called them to my mother's attention, she admonished me for telling "lies." Occasionally I would awaken from vivid flying dreams and ask her when we had exchanged our wings for legs. Sometimes I would pause in confusion at mealtime and wonder why we had to eat living creatures when breathing alone should suffice. Because these comments seemed to terrify my mother and drove a deeper wedge between us, I soon learned to keep them to myself.

Anthropologist Ruth Montgomery's observation about Western culture made over 60 years ago—"Even a very mild mystic is aberrant in our culture" (1934, p. 59)—is as accurate today as it was then. When folklorist Gillian Bennet (1987) interviewed 107 women in Great Britain about their spiritual experiences, she had to adapt the wording of her questions and prompts to fit in with the phraseology the women themselves used.

> For example, I found early on that I had to drop terms like "the supernatural" altogether; for my informants it was not a neutral, nor even a factual term; its connotations were wholly evil and taboo. As long as I said I was doing research on "the supernatural," I had only negative reactions, ranging from denial to hostility and even real fear. As soon as I took to speaking in a vague fashion about "the mysterious side of life," the women relented, showed decided interest, and were eager to talk. (p. 26)

Ian Stevenson (1987) found that some of the families in his research cohort were quite accepting of their children's past life recall, even when their memories upset the family balance, but others were confused, fearful, and occasionally hostile. The differences in their responses depended less on their particular religious beliefs than on their psychological comfort with the spiritual realm (although occasionally they feared that the child might be laying claim to another family's property or status). Andrija Puharich (1974), another physician, recounted a negative memory of one of his patients.

One day when Harry was about six years old he suddenly announced to his mother that a favorite aunt was dying at the moment in the hospital and would be dead shortly. The mother sternly upbraided him for such a wild suggestion and put him to bed. That evening, about six hours later, the family received word that the aunt had been stuck by a car and had died in a hospital. After this the parents became quite concerned about their son, Harry. Being devout Catholics, they, of course, went to the parish priest for advice. Because of this experience and other like experiences, Harry says he was lectured to many times by his parish priest about the desirability of avoiding them since this clearly was the temptation of the devil. Over the years Harry had had instilled into him the idea that any such experience was evil and bad for one's soul, and was to be avoided at all costs. (pp. 39-40)

Children are not the only people discouraged from visiting the spiritual realm. Scientists who wish to study these phenomena must still do so cautiously. When I was conducting my dissertation research into the psychological effects of transcendent experiences during the mid-1980s, one of my professors confessed that were he to openly admit to an interest in the subject, he would be committing professional suicide. More recently, my continuing interest in this area threatened my academic career when colleagues debated the legitimacy of this kind of inquiry. And I know scientists in many disciplines who are interested in consciousness and spirituality but are loath to make their interest public, for fear of collegial scorn.

Why do these experiences cause so many people so much discomfort? It is impossible to trace the reasons to a single source. There are, however, three factors that I believe contribute powerfully to individual and institutional disquiet: the tendency of organized religions to enforce conformity and to silence conflicting subjective experience through means that are often ruthless; the use of science to combat religious oppression by confining our focus to physical phenomena; and the intellectual and emotional distress evoked by the idea that physical existence is the tip of the iceberg of consciousness. Each of these issues is explored next.

THE DEMONIZATION OF THE UNCONSCIOUS

Religious oppression is rampant in human history. Indeed, there does not seem to be an age when some group of believers wasn't attempting to impose its particular cosmology on another. Five thousand years ago a gradual and widespread patriarchal revolution transformed the Great Mother religions into Great Father traditions, triggering a global, catastrophic, and continuing devaluation of women (Stone, 1978). One thousand years ago a series of bloody confrontations between Christianity and Islam led to the Children's Crusade in which thousands of children died or were sold into slavery attempting to recapture Christ's Sepulcher in Jerusalem (Tuchman, 1978). Eight hundred years ago, the witchcraft persecutions in Western Europe began and resulted in the legalized murder of thousands of women and men (Kors & Peters, 1972). Five hundred years ago, Spain, Portugal, France, Holland, Belgium, and England colonized the indigenous peoples of Africa and the Americas, resulting in genocide, slavery, and the suppression of nature-based religions. Sixty years ago the German Third Reich exterminated 6,000,000 Jews. In the 1970s, the takeover of Iran by Islamic fundamentalists led to the exile, persecution, and execution of secular Iranians and moderate Muslims. Salmon Rushdie, an Indian writer now living in New York City, went into hiding to escape a sentence of death issued by the Ayatollah Khomeni for his novel about the Prophet Mohammed. More recently, feminist theologian Susan Brooks Thistlethwaite received numerous death threats from members of the American Christian Right for helping to translate the Bible into contemporary, gender-inclusive language. And Afghan women have lost their rights to education, work, and free access to public space since the recent takeover of their country by Taliban fundamentalists.

Prejudice, fear, ignorance, and hatred, masquerading as religious belief, have powerfully shaped humankind's relationship to spirituality. One of the most graphic and far-reaching examples is the persecution of witches that dominated the intellectual, social, and spiritual life of Western Europe for almost 700 years, reaching epidemic and ultimately cataclysmic proportions. A brief history of this tragic epoch illustrates how powerfully its legacy continues to haunt us.

When the Roman Empire began to disintegrate in the early years of the Common Era, the Roman Catholic Church rose to take its place, gradually becoming the principle source of intellectual, spiritual, and moral authority across the whole of Western Europe. All institutions establish rules of belief and exact penalties from those who disagree or disobey, and the Church was no exception. As Christianity coalesced into a major political power, contending factions jockeyed for power and for the right to determine dogma. In the waning years of the Roman Empire, for example, many Gnostics (who believed in reincarnation, the equality of women, and the abandonment of a priestly hierarchy) were literally thrown to the lions by those calling themselves Orthodox Christians, who were then able to dominate the emerging Church (Pagels, 1979).

The silencing of dissent took other forms once the Roman Empire collapsed. The accusation of heresy became a potent instrument of social control during the Church's first thousand years, albeit not the lethal weapon it would become 100 years later. There are records indicating that as early as the fifth century, an Irish monk named Pelagius was censured by the Latin hierarchy in Rome for professing his belief in the inseparability of spirit and flesh. Whereas Church Fathers saw physical reality as a necessary evil on the road to eternal life, Pelagius argued "that the secret of the state of creative being lies in achieving a balance between inner revelation and outward manifestation. . . . The ideal should be to actualize the individual self as fully as possible while learning how to live and die as a servant, at one with the universe" (quoted in Fox, 1981, p. 181). Pelagius was condemned as a heretic, excommunicated, and exiled from Rome, his theological contributions vanishing from Catholic theosophy.

The consolidation of the Christian empire, which began in the first centuries of the Common Era, took increasingly virulent shape after 1100. Sorcery and witchcraft had been practiced throughout Europe for centuries before this period, but they were not considered a deadly threat until the Church began to systematize and codify its teachings into a coherent body of theology and canonical law. After 1100, Church officials began to actively seek out and punish anyone believed to be a "servant of Satan" and a threat to the continuation of Christian Europe. When the secular courts came under the Church's sway, the witchcraft persecutions began in earnest.

The Inquisition, which masterminded this religious reign of terror, began its existence as a political tool to further the economic soundness of Catholic Spain by driving the Jews and Moors from its borders. As a tribunal of the Roman Catholic Church, however, its stated purpose was to suppress "heresy." In 1258, the Inquisitors asked Pope Alexander IV for permission to add witchcraft to the list of ecclesiastical offenses over which they had jurisdiction. Alexander agreed, but "only if there was evidence of manifest heresy in their cases. This was the point at which Inquisitors, theologians, and canonical lawyers began to find means of identifying witchcraft with heresy" (Kors & Peters, 1972, p. 77).

At the base of what was to become a vicious and long-running conflict lay the debate over the relationship of the spiritual to the physical world. Those who argued that the goal of life was to negate the body, glorify the spirit, and aspire to eternal life were the Inquisitors; those who argued that the body and spirit were inseparable facets of each other were labeled witches and heretics; those who defended the accused or who argued that this argument was ridiculous were condemned as accomplices of Satan.

Even such Church luminaries as Thomas Aquinas (1223-1274) and Meister Eckhart (1260-1327) were not exempt from persecution. Thomas Aquinas argued that nature was not a mere shadow of the supernatural but contained spiritual energies in itself. "To study nature and existence was for Aquinas a form of prayer and meditation, indeed a 'liturgy' as he insisted in his running debates with cloistered monks of his day" (Fox, 1981, p. 193). Not only did Thomas insist on the inseparability of spirit and matter, as had Pelagius some 800 years earlier, but he also advocated the attainment of spirituality through "delight" rather than law. "If we become spiritual only by an imperative issuing from reason and will," Thomas said, "virtue is in some way forced. It lacks of harmony with the nature of passion. It would proceed with repugnance and frustration that leads to sadness instead of blossoming into a state of delight" (p. 197). Shortly before his death these beliefs were condemned as heresy. Although Thomas Aquinas was canonized in 1323, his approach to spirituality never took hold. As Fox observed, "Thomas Aquinas paid dearly for his holism and so too has Christian spirituality since his time" (pp. 199-200).

Meister Eckhart, a great mystic and Dominican scholar who laid the foundations of German philosophy and mysticism, also fell into disgrace for insisting that "all that is is holy." Not only did he argue that the separation of physical and spiritual reality was an illusion, but he insisted that spirituality did not require the convoluted rules and regulations propounded by the hierarchy in Rome. Meister Eckhart's arguments ran afoul of the Inquisition, which pronounced them heretical as well as wrong, and though he escaped excommunication and execution, he was shunned.

From the vantage point of the twentieth century, it is impossible to appreciate the extent to which fear of Satanism dominated every facet of medieval life, but, in fact, the word "devil" was as much a part of their vernacular as "virus" is of ours. Between 1100 and 1700, Christianity was the detailed, common frame of reference that united Europe. Everyone who occupied an ecclesiastical, scholarly, or judicial position upheld this belief system as the literal blueprint of God's creation. All religions must account for evil and catastrophe in some way; medieval Christianity gave devils and witches a logically consistent place much as Hitler demonized the Jews to justify Nazism, and Khomeni demonized the West to excuse the excesses of his Islamic revolution. After Gutenberg invented the printing press in 1454, an increasingly literate public emerged. Then, with the publication of the enormously influential *Malleus Mallificarum* (*Hammer of Witches*) in 1486, "Europe's concern over the nature, activities, and numbers of witches became a dominant intellectual, emotional, ecclesiastical and juridical preoccupation of men from all walks of life" (Kors & Peters, 1972, p. 4). The *Malleus*, written by two Dominican monks, was the most detailed treatise on witchcraft to appear. It argued that women were more likely than men to be witches and justified the ruling that opposition and skepticism were punishable by torture and death: "The belief that there are such beings as witches is so essential a part of the Catholic faith that obstinately to maintain the opposite opinion manifestly savors of heresy" (p. 11).

The social, political, and economic turbulence of the fourteenth and fifteenth centuries overwhelmed the European psyche. Incessant warfare and severe climatic shifts resulted in widespread famine and poverty, the Black Plague decimated one-third of Europe's population, and a pervasive sense of helplessness and terror informed scholarly, theological, and popular thought. As Christendom splintered into the venomous factions that would result in the Reformation and Counter-Reformation of the sixteenth century, as recurring episodes of plague and famine ravaged the population, and as the old feudal order convulsed and died, thousands of hapless women and men were scapegoated as "the visible agents of evil upon the earth" (Kors & Peters, 1982, p. 6).

It is, of course, impossible to discuss the witchcraft persecutions without acknowledging the hatred of women that fueled and exacerbated their viciousness. From 1100 until 1785, hundreds of thousands of people were tortured and executed as "servants of Satan," 50 women to every 1 man. The wise women and men who had served their villages and towns as herbalists, midwives, healers, and counselors were gradually transformed into fiendish witches and wizards. So, eventually, were neighbors whose dogs barked too loudly, the elderly whom family members could no longer afford to feed, the feeble-minded who had once been cared for communally, and anyone who denied a charge of witchcraft, defended an accused, or argued that the Inquisition had gone too far. The heresies for which people were prosecuted included the belief that children should not be baptized until they reached the age of reason or consent, opposition to the selling of prayers for the dead or indulgences for the living, and rejection of the concept of purgatory. Joan of Arc was excommunicated by the Church and executed by the State in 1433 as much for wearing men's clothing as for acting on the mystical visions that compelled her to reunite France. Eventually, the sentencing to death of entire villages was not unknown.

The Reformation, which began in 1517 with Martin Luther's protest against the excesses of the Catholic Church, greatly intensified the crisis of witchcraft. Protestants placed an even greater emphasis on the scriptural Satan and the Old Testament injunction of Exodus 22:18—"Thou shalt not suffer a witch to live"—than did Catholic Europe. Luther extended the scope of persecution by arguing not only that witchcraft was heresy, but that all false Biblical interpretation was witchcraft. Meanwhile, in Switzerland, Jean Calvin was insisting "that the Bible had either literally described men possessed by or in service to Satan, or offered meaningless statements about the nature of God's universe; the latter, of course, was unacceptable" (Zilboorg, 1941, p. 193). A casualty of this new Protestant dogmatism was a Norfolk plowright who was burned at the stake in 1578 for suggesting that the New Testament was just a story of men.

As Protestantism swept Europe and vied with Catholicism for intellectual, spiritual, and political dominance, the persecutions escalated to appalling dimensions. Protestants accused the Catholic clergy of fostering witchcraft through "popish blasphemies," and Catholics proceeded to identify witchcraft with Protestantism itself. The conflagration ignited by Luther raced across the European Continent, jumped the English Channel and the North Sea, and erupted in relatively untouched England and Scotland. It then leapt across the Atlantic Ocean to the British Colonies in North America, where it fueled the hysteria that led to the witch trials in Salem, Massachusetts, in 1692.

> No estate, no class, no group was completely exempt from the pervasiveness of belief in witchcraft and the even more dangerous belief that anyone could be a witch and that witches could strike anywhere. The theological and judicial portrait of the witch responded to and inspired in its turn an ever-widening public consensus until scholar and peasant, jurist and artisan, priest and layman, king and merchant, all believed, and believing, feared and called for even more intense persecution. (Kors & Peters, 1972, p. 12)

It is easy to look back and shake one's head at the insanity and devastation wrought by that long debate about spiritual reality, much as the characters on Star Trek often remarked on the ignorance and brutality of the twentieth century from their vantage point in the twenty-fourth century. But like the bacteria that caused the Black Death, the terror of those times is still with us. It was the basis of Harry's mother's fear and that of my great-aunt's priest. Many years ago I awoke from an agonizing dream, drenched in sweat and shaking with fear. In my dream I was a small, gray cloud of consciousness hiding behind a screaming mob, whispering "Don't let them find me, don't let them do that to me again!" After people began to disperse I saw the remains of 40 women smoldering at the base of 40 stakes. Although I rarely discuss this dream, I have been struck by how often clients report

similar dreams and by the frequency with which intellectual opposition to spirituality is linked to fears of religious persecution.

In the mid-seventeenth century, the beliefs that had
formed the social and intellectual life of Europe for almost 700
years abruptly began to collapse. Although the last witches were
legally burned in Europe in 1785, there was ultimately no body of
clerical, legal, or professional authority willing to lead, justify, or
defend such practices.

> By the dawn of the eighteenth century, the question was no
> longer whether Christian belief demanded a belief in witch-
> craft . . . but whether the system which had generated and
> compelled such beliefs could continue to hold any authority
> over the minds and hearts of thinking men. With that ques-
> tion, the men of the eighteenth century led European civiliza-
> tion into another age, and as Voltaire remarked, the witches
> and exorcists both, if they remained quiet, would be left in
> peace. (Kors & Peters, 1972, p. 310)

THE SCIENTIFIC SOLUTION

All belief systems tend to overcorrect when they have gone too
far in one direction. When the new age turned from spiritual-
ism to materialism, a fundamental shift occurred in the way reality was perceived and explored. For the first time, physical reality
became the focus of scientific and intellectual attention. In part,
this was because the physical realm was (and is) an endless
source of fascination—particularly when explorers no longer
faced the threat of episcopal condemnation. But I believe a less-
conscious reason was also involved.

As the collective certainty in Satan's desire to vanquish
the Christian world evaporated, educated men increasingly
sought to distance themselves from the "credulity" and "superstition" that had fueled the madness of the preceding centuries. Of
course, not everyone benefited from this new way of thinking. The
question of whether women had souls (now called intellects) continued to be hotly debated, and most were kept out of school in
the interest of furthering their appeal as wives and domestics.
The countries of Europe were racing to colonize the countries of

Africa and the Americas, and Christianity, though no longer engaged in the persecution of witches, was now used to justify the oppression of indigenous peoples and the theft of their lands. Demonological explanations of natural phenomena were replaced by new epistomologies that eschewed theology and relied instead on strict observation, empirical testing of all hypotheses, and a critical rationalism. Science swept through all segments of society and all schools of thought, displacing the witch-fear that had embedded itself in Europe's psyche. The age-old conflict between spiritual and physical interpretations of reality was still alive and well, but the balance of power now shifted to the physical side of the equation.

Although there had been intimations of this new way of thinking in the distant past, notably the astronomical observations of Nicholaus Copernicus (1473-1543) and Galileo Galilei (1564-1642), "the old world would not surrender willingly [and] the new world just born was too young to fight a winning battle" (Zilboorg, 1941, p. 246). Following the dictum "Cogito ergo sum" of French mathematician and philosopher Rene Descartes (1596-1650), intellectual attention became increasingly riveted on the physical world. With Descartes' explanation that "nothing exists in the whole of nature that cannot be explained in terms of purely corporeal causes," so began the scientific revolution. The demonological beliefs that had formed the core of seven centuries of intellectual life were now dismissed by Benjamin Spinoza, Thomas Hobbes, and other then-contemporary thinkers as philosophical naivete and sectarian spats about the nature of God. In the eighteenth century, the universe became a great machine that ran itself without supernatural intervention. No spiritual being, dimension, or process was required to explain the existence of the earth, its inhabitants, or its events; any phenomena that could not be explained on the basis of known or emerging physical laws were dismissed as unworthy of thought.

> Whatever his guise, ecclesiastical or secular, [the scientist] seemed to prefer to consider least matters which concerned the nature of his mind. The more pervasive his curiosity, the more he became preoccupied with things outside himself. . . . The scientist was coming into his own, and he was preoccupied with the magnitude of his task: to steal as many secrets as possible from nature. (Zilboorg, 1941, pp. 247-248)

As the last of the witches were being set alight, the great European science academies were born, and members soon began to publish scientific reports. Some were prosecuted by the Inquisition, but that once all-powerful tribunal was rapidly losing the control that had caused Galileo to recant his astronomical observations or face execution. The new explorers, enamored with the systematic investigation of physical reality, demanded and invented new, more sophisticated instruments with which to do so. The microscope, thermometer, barometer, and steam engine came into being; magnetism and electricity began to be studied; science was differentiated into anatomy, physiology, chemistry, biology, physics, mathematics, and neurology. Finance and economics began to be developed as practical, political, and empirical disciplines. Even the stake was replaced by a modern method of mass destruction in France. No longer were people executed for possession and witchcraft, however; those who defended the collapsing feudal order or insisted on outmoded ways of thinking were now denounced as enemies to the newly emerging state and guillotined.

The medieval ecclesiastical world may have rejected Copernicus' claim that the earth revolved around the sun, but the emerging scientific world displayed a similar propensity for small-mindedness, particularly in the field of medicine from which psychology emerged. "The appearance of any innovation or discovery in medicine . . . was more or less hissed down as a matter of emotional tradition. An innovator was never welcome and hardly ever treated politely" (Zilboorg, 1941, p. 352). The scientific hierarchy greeted new and initially incomprehensible ideas with as much fear and hostility as the Church had shown during the heyday of demonology. Members of the Paris Academie scoffed at Louis Pasteur when he first reported the medical discoveries that led to the recognition of infectious disease. E.G. Elliotson, the first physician in England to use a stethoscope, was considered a radical and a disturber of the medical peace by the foremost teachers of his day, and his stethoscope derided as an object of superstition and contempt. Despite his own inventive genius, Thomas Edison argued vehemently that George Westinghouse's licensure and promotion of the alternating current discovered by Nikola Tesla would have disastrous consequences for all who used it to light up their homes. It may be hard to remember, but vaccinations, airplanes, personal computers, and space exploration were also once the stuff of scientific derision and/or fiction.

It was in this climate that the discipline of psychology was born, a field that has had enormous influence over the way we now view spiritual events. The word "scientific" had long since become synonymous with "organic," "physiological," and "corporeal." Medicine had chosen to confine itself to describing and conquering disease, not inquiring into the nature of the psyche or the spirit. The scientific world, still running from the demonological debacle, was never comfortable with psychology because it concerned itself with issues that had long been associated with the soul and the devil. Some scientists even described the emerging discipline as the "devil in modern dress" (Zilboorg, 1941, p. 355). To gain credibility as a scientific discipline, psychology had to divorce itself from any suggestion that it was still living in Satan's shadow. This it did by adapting itself to the experimental research methods developed in the fields of physics, chemistry, and physiology, and by focusing on practical, quantifiable, and empirically testable questions that could be asked—and answered—in laboratory situations. The mind was identified with the brain, its behavior said to be regulated by and limited to physical systems. Any paranormal or spiritual experience was attributed to disease, injury, oxygen deprivation, or gullibility. After the eighteenth century, whatever scientific interest remained in the supernatural went largely underground. The problem was, the mystery of spiritual phenomena could not be so easily dismissed.

In 1778, Franz Anton Mesmer brought his discovery of "animal magnetism" to public attention. Mesmer claimed that stars influenced human beings through the flow of a magnetic fluid that linked the universe with the human body. In order for humans to remain physically and mentally healthy, the harmony of this balance needed to be maintained by a "magnetizer who could . . . initiate a greater flow of the magnetic fluid into or from the patient through contact with him or even at a distance" (Zilboorg, 1941, p. 347). From the outset, mesmerism suffered because of its association with precisely those elements from which psychology was trying so desperately to flee—the spirit, the soul, and by extension, the devil. Because he was unable to offer any plausible scientific explanation for his clinical data, and because he had an unbridled penchant for flamboyance and self-aggrandizement, Mesmer quickly fell into disgrace. But mesmerism slowly percolated through medical and psychological circles and eventually "led to a totally new orientation which brought psychotherapy to the forefront and with it, ultimately, the deepest insight yet attained by man into the inner workings of the human mind" (p. 378).

In 1843, the term *mesmerism* was transformed into *hypnotism* by James Braid, an English surgeon who was convinced, on the basis of his own studies, that some underlying, albeit obscure psychological process was involved that was decidedly *not* of the devil. Over the next 30 years, hypnotism became an increasingly popular source of scientific speculation and experimentation throughout Europe and England. One particularly inquisitive mind belonged to Jean Martin Charcot, a nineteenth-century French neurologist, who subsequently found a brilliant, articulate, and revolutionary pupil in Sigmund Freud.

Freud was one of the first modern scientists to use clinical, empirical, descriptive, and phenomenological techniques to study the mind. He introduced the study of anthropology into psychology and invented psychoanalysis and psychotherapy as research methodologies, thereby allowing patients to describe their own subjective, psychological states. Freud created a unique topography of the unconscious and argued that dreams were not pathological symptoms but phenomena of normal mental life that occurred in any healthy person. However innovative his psychological insights were, however, Freud's theories were firmly grounded in the physical world—particularly in neurology and physiology. At no point did he speak of the mind in theological or philosophical terms. Even so, his ideas met with an extraordinary degree of resistance.

> Man could not accept gratefully that there is an unconscious. To admit that he might act without knowing why and yet be in full possession of his senses meant to admit the existence within himself of something normally inaccessible to his mind. . . . Admission means acknowledgement of an enormous, rich, complex, and unknown life within us of which we are seldom or never aware. (Zilboorg, 1941, pp. 487-488)

Throughout his life Freud complained bitterly that his theories were dismissed as "unscientific" because he was dealing with subjective rather than objective states. He argued, for example, that

> Zoology and botany did not start from correct and adequate definitions of an animal and a plant; to this very day biology has been unable to give any certain meaning to the concept of life. Physics itself . . . would never have made any advance if it had to wait until its concepts of matter, force, gravitation, and so on, had reached the desirable degree of clarity and precision. (1935, pp. 117-118)

Fear and ignorance lay at the basis of his rejection. As Francis Bacon lamented 400 years earlier, "man prefers to believe what he prefers to be true," a statement that is as appropriate to Freud's time and our own as it was to the sixteenth century.

All people have their psychological blind spots against which genius is no protection. Much of the vehemence Freud brought to his biological theories of psychological functioning derived from his strong objection to religion's "unwholesome effect" on human consciousness. Freud argued that the concept of God, modeled on the human father and rooted in the relationship between father and child, was projected onto the universe and then deified. He saw religion as an intrinsically pathological and universal obsessional neurosis: belief in God was a form of immaturity that reflected a person's inability to turn early sexual desires into mature adult attitudes. In a letter to his colleague C.G. Jung, Freud begged him "never to abandon the sexual theory. That is the most essential thing of all. You see we must make a dogma of it, an unshakable bulwark . . . against the black tide of occultism" (Jung, 1965, p. 150). This belief is still reflected in psychoanalytic thought, with some contemporary psychiatrists arguing, for example, that "mystical states represent regressions to very early periods of infancy. The basic characteristic-that of ecstatic union-suggests a regression to early nursing experiences" (Prince & Savage, 1972, p. 127).

Carl Jung, initially a disciple and friend of Freud's, broke with his mentor in large part because of Freud's prejudice against spiritual experience, a position with which Jung emphatically disagreed. "Anyone who has had it is *seized* by it and therefore not in a position to indulge in fruitless metaphysical or epistemological speculations" (Jung, 1965, p. 91; emphasis in original). The problem was not that spirituality was inherently neurotic or pathological but that humans unconsciously imposed all their own neuroses and psychopathologies on their concepts of the Divine.

Jung was deeply concerned that psychology would be encased within biology and believed that it needed a radical revolution, "in the same way that our misconceptions of the solar system had to be freed from prejudice by Copernicus," to free psychology from the prejudice that it was "a mere epiphenomenon of a biochemical process in the brain" (Jung, 1958, p. 45). This was a revolution that Jung was uniquely qualified to lead by virtue of his medical training, his multidisciplinary orientation, and his own spiritual encounters. Following a series of extraordinary visions in 1944, for example, he realized that "life is a segment of existence which is enacted in a three-dimensional boxlike universe especially set up for it" (1965, p. 295). The rest of his professional life was devoted to exploring the psychological territories beyond the box. "Most people confuse 'self-knowledge' with knowledge of their conscious ego personalities," Jung wrote shortly before he died. "But the ego knows only its own contents, not the unconscious and its contents" (1965, p. 7). To Jung, anyone who practiced psychology or any other science while ignoring the existence of spiritual phenomena was "intellectually lazy and scientifically irresponsible." Denial, he held, was simply "a popular way out of a quite extraordinary intellectual difficulty" (1965, p. 45).

Spiritual experiences not only present us with an extraordinary intellectual difficulty but with an extraordinary *emotional* difficulty. They require us to suspend the belief that the physical world is all there is, all that matters, or "more basic than nonmaterial reality" (Weil, 1972, p. 130). This is asking much in a scientific climate that overwhelmingly views this stance as imaginary or psychotic. Because spiritual experiences are departures from one's ordinary state of consciousness and conflict powerfully with Western ideas about reality, many people ignore, avoid, or dismiss them for fear of being thought crazy. As Michael Murphy (1992) said, "To explore the terra incognita of our latent capacities, we must love adventure, complexity, and strange territory" (p. 581). Some eschew this territory because they believe that only saints or the insane would willingly go where few have gone before, or because they fear the loss of their psychological bearings in an unfathomable spiritual sea. This fear is "often . . . so great that one dares not admit it even to oneself" (Jung, 1958, p. 49). Spiritual experiences cannot be induced by reason nor fully understood by the intellect, only interpreted once they occur. As the medieval mystic Meister Eckhart observed, these experiences "cannot be accomplished by will power or by intellect power. The process is by definition the surrendering of power, and with it a surrendering of our images and all preconceptions of things as we think they are" (quoted in Fox, 1981, p. 227). For those who have grown up under the long shadow of Descartes, this can be a terrifying proposition, one that leads humankind to seesaw periodically between extremes of scientific materialism and religious fundamentalism.

Another reason for the discomfort is the inability to reconcile spiritual experiences within the paradigm defined by contemporary Western science. As Thomas Kuhn remarked, "No part of the aim of normal science is to call forth new sorts of phenomena; indeed, those that will not fit the box are often not seen at all" (1962, p. 24). But increasing numbers of scientists on the other side of the debate argue that the existence of these phenomena is evidence that the current scientific paradigm itself is wrong (e.g., Brophy, 1999; Mitchell, 1974; Radin, 1997; Wolman, 1977). Indeed, H. J. Eysenck, former head of the Department of Psychology at Maudsley Hospital in London, proposed that those who were the most skeptical about spirituality were the most ignorant of the facts.

> Unless there is a gigantic conspiracy involving 30 university departments all over the world, and several hundred highly respected scientists in various fields, many of them originally hostile to the claims of psychic researchers, the only conclusion the unbiased observer can come to must be that there are people who obtain knowledge existing either in other people's minds, or in the outer world, by means yet unknown to science. (quoted in Mitchell, 1974, p. 47)

It is fashionable in some circles to dismiss spirituality as charlatanism or "New Age." Yet, the central spiritual premise—"that the universe is not a dead machine but a living presence, that in its essence and tendency it is infinitely good, and that individual existence is continuous beyond what is called death" (Bucke, 1972, p. 79)—is hardly spiritual snake oil, however much hyperbole and silliness occasionally surrounds it. It is, instead, a premise that has guided the thinking of humankind's most gifted philosophers and teachers, one for which "human beings have—throughout history—sacrificed peace of mind, comfort of body, and often life itself" (LeShan, 1990, p. 87). Spiritual phenomena might be difficult for some people to accept and for others to prove, but that does not mean they are false. Nor does it mean that those who experience such phenomena are regressing to the infantile or the irrational. The fact that so many people are acknowledging the importance of spirituality may signify that we have reached a critical point in the development of the human species and that it is time to bring a deeper level of awareness to our lives for our own sake and that of future generations.

CHAPTER THREE

In Search of Spiritual Intelligence

The point of unusual experiences is, as a rule, not so much to answer questions as to open them. They stir us out of our habitual assumptions.
—Richard Woods (1981)

In his classic science fiction novel, *Childhood's End*, Arthur C. Clarke (1953) proposed an intriguing solution to the psychosocial problems that are ravaging humankind. An advanced extraterrestrial civilization, frustrated with the refusal of the human race to grow up and cease destroying itself and the planet, appeared one day over the major cities of the world, unilaterally destroying all weapons of individual and mass destruction and taking over the administration of daily affairs. Their purpose was not to colonize the Earth but to begin the transformation of human consciousness that would permit its greater interaction with the universal "Overmind."

As tempting as it is to think that something other than ourselves will save humanity from its follies, that is unlikely to occur. Yet, the leap of consciousness envisioned by Clarke may well be underway. The primary spiritual insight, that "our inner life is many-dimensional, multilayered, and teeming with presences of various kinds" (Murphy, 1992, p. 559), lies at the heart of every culture's faith tradition and creation myth. In recent years, this awareness has captured the attention of the general public as never before. Ever since consciousness-altering drugs became popular among the North American counter-culture in the 1960s, larger numbers of people have been encountering spiritual realities for the first time. Unprecedented advances in medical technology have enabled millions of children and adults to return from the threshold of death, many of whom describe life-changing encounters in spiritual realms (Morse, 1990, 1994; Ring, 1984). Popular films and television programs such as *Resurrection* and *The X Files* have explored the farther reaches of human consciousness, and Eastern spiritual disciplines such as yoga and meditation have become common practices in secular Western organizations. And people from all faith traditions in increasing numbers are embracing nontraditional forms of worship that emphasize spiritual transformation.

Science has also shown a marked interest in the reach of consciousness. Theoretical physicists like David Bohm (Weber, 1986), Fritzjof Capra (1975), and Norman Friedman (1990) have written eloquently about the similarities between quantum and mystical insights. A growing number of interdisciplinary centers (e.g., the Fetzer Institute, the Institute for the Scientific Study of Subtle Energies, the National Institute of Health-Office of Alternative Medicine, The Interdisciplinary Research Committee on Consciousness Studies at the University of Washington, and the Consciousness Studies Program at the University of Arizona) are actively exploring the intersection of science and spirit. The extraordinary growth of plants at the Scottish spiritual community, Findhorn, induced botanists to study plant responses to the energy of human thought (Tompkins & Bird, 1973). Rupert Sheldrake's (1988) theory of morphic resonance led to biological examinations of the telepathic exchange of information among various animal populations. Engineers like Robert Monroe (1977, 1985) studied the psychophysiology of out-of-body experiences, and nursing students are regularly taught "therapeutic touch," a new term for the ancient healing art of the "laying on of hands." Hypnosis, once considered the stuff of magic shows and seances, has become standard practice in psychotherapy and behavioral medicine.

What accounts for this explosive new interest in ancient spiritual matters? According to Evelyn Underhill (1911), a preeminent scholar of mysticism, the Western world has witnessed a marked increase in spiritual activity at the end of every period of great change. Epochs such as the second century, the Middle Ages, and the Renaissance brought extraordinary innovation and cultural realignment to human populations and closed with a surge in spiritual consciousness. This was not the sort of apocalyptic behavior practiced throughout the centuries by various religious sects, but an enthusiastic exploration of the spiritual realm and a "remaking of character about new and higher centers of life" (p. 446).

When one observes the phenomenal innovations that have occurred in virtually every sphere of human activity over the past century, it is not surprising that this pattern should be repeating itself in our own time. From in-vitro fertilization to genetic engineering, from biplanes to the Space Shuttle, from television to the internet, from the extension of civil rights to women and people of color in the United States to the end of apartheid in South Africa, this has been an age of technological wonders and unparalleled social transformation. Unfortunately, some of our wildest dreams have turned into inconceivable nightmares: nuclear proliferation, ethnic cleansing, ecological devastation, and the increasing use of assault weapons by children are but a few. Whether humankind will awaken from these nightmares before an irreversible global catastrophe occurs is the subject of Clarke's book and the critical psychological issue of our time. Such an awakening is possible, I believe, but only if we bring a new depth of consciousness or *spiritual intelligence* to our individual and collective lives.

WHAT IS SPIRITUAL INTELLIGENCE?

There is an ancient Hindu metaphor that captures the essence of spiritual intelligence. Imagine that the conscious or waking self is like water in a glass in the middle of the ocean. The ocean symbolizes the "Universe," or what some call "God," "Creator," or "All That Is." The glass represents the psychological lens through which we perceive both inner and outer worlds. The goal of spiritual intelligence is to expand the borders of the glass while simultaneously increasing its translucence and permeability.

Spiritual intelligence is an innate human potential, but like any talent or gift it is expressed in various ways and to various degrees throughout the human population. As Hollingworth (1914, 1926), Gardner (1993), and Getzells and Csikszentmihalyi (1976), among others, have shown, intelligence includes the capacity to think, to plan, to create, to translate ideas into reality, to adapt to changing circumstances, to find and solve problems, to reflect on and communicate well with self and others, and to grow from mistakes. Emmons (1999) reviewed the empirical literature in the psychology of religion and spirituality and identified five core characteristics that he associated with spiritual intelligence: "the capacity to transcend the physical and material; the ability to experience heightened states of consciousness; the ability to sanctify everyday experiences; the ability to utilize spiritual resources to solve problems; and the capacity to be virtuous" (p. 164). Although my research largely agrees with Emmons' review, I believe that spiritual intelligence includes two additional, critical abilities. The first is the conscious recognition that physical reality is embedded within a larger, multidimensional reality with which we interact, consciously and unconsciously, on a moment-to-moment basis. The second is the conscious pursuit of psychological health, not only for ourselves but for the sake of the global community. In the following pages I illustrate how and why these are important components.

Spiritual intelligence is a dynamic and fluid process, not a static product. It includes *but is not limited to* openness to the kinds of spiritual phenomena described in Chapter One. Although these experiences can be exciting and challenging, they do not automatically bring about psychological growth. In order for them to quicken that growth we must be open to perceiving them; assessing their physical, psychological, and interpersonal impact; and integrating them intelligently into our lives. *Intelligence* is the critical part of this equation. This is neither blind nor rigid adherence to a prescribed set of beliefs, but a mindset that tolerates uncertainty and paradox as well as the anxiety of "not knowing." Although an individual might choose to practice a particular religion or spiritual discipline, spiritual intelligence is the awareness that the whole is always greater than the sum of its parts, no matter how cherished a part might be.

SPIRITUAL INTELLIGENCE AND PSYCHOLOGICAL HEALTH

How does spiritual intelligence promote psychological development? This is a question I have been pondering for many years, but there are no easy answers. The story of St. Francis of Assisi demonstrates how different spirituality can look depending on one's point of view.

Francis was born in 1182 to a wealthy Italian family and, as an indulged and cherished son, he soon acquired an appetite for luxury, fine clothes, and perpetual amusement. He was also drawn to poetry and music and shrank from ugliness in any form, although occasionally he would go among the poor, giving alms to beggars and lepers. One day, when he was 24 years of age, Francis walked past a small church in Assisi and felt a surprising compulsion to enter and pray. As soon as he knelt before the altar he was overcome by a spiritual experience that completely rearranged his psychological universe. "Smitten by unwonted visitations, [Francis] found himself another man than he who had gone in. There are no hesitations, no uncertainties. The change, which he cannot describe, he knows to be central for life" (Underhill, 1911, pp. 180-181).

Within a short period of time, Francis renounced materialism and began to give large amounts of family money to various religious groups. His horrified father, finding his protests falling on deaf ears, subjected Francis to house arrest and physical punishment in an effort to return him to his former self. Finally, he sued his son for the money that Francis had given away. The court upheld the father's demand for restitution, whereupon Francis returned not only the money but all the clothing he was wearing. He then walked out of court and joined a religious community, eventually founding an order that was dedicated to serving the needs of the poor. In time he was canonized by the Roman Catholic Church and became one of its most beloved saints. As two psychologists who studied St. Francis' life, observed,

> The case of St. Francis suggests how difficult it can be to determine whether transcendent experience is a force for mental health or for sickness. St. Francis acted in ways that many would consider signs of mental illness, and yet many would consider him one of the most psychologically whole, healthy people who ever lived. (Batson & Ventis, 1982, p. 212)

I sat with a friend one rainy afternoon drinking tea and debating whether spiritual intelligence helps or hinders psychological growth. My friend is a wise and brilliant psychiatrist who is deeply committed to her own and others' health. We agree on most psychological issues, except when it comes to the role of spirituality. My friend describes herself as a contented atheist and rejects the validity of spiritual experiences, arguing that they can easily be explained as hallucinations or delusions resulting from temporal lobe seizures, anoxia, or psychosis. Besides, she asked, what difference does spirituality make as long as people function well in their lives?

My friend makes a valid point. Certainly, one can be psychologically healthy, live a productive life, have meaningful relationships, and treat others well without a conscious awareness of spirituality. Certainly, spiritual experiences can sometimes be induced in the laboratory through drugs or electrical stimulation to specific parts of the brain and have little, if anything, to do with spiritual intelligence. And certainly there are abundant examples of humans who commit heinous crimes in support of their religious or spiritual beliefs and who cannot be considered psychologically healthy by most people's criteria. Admittedly, I am hard-pressed to resolve these contradictions. Yet, as I watched some people integrate their spiritual awareness into the totality of their lives and observed their growing resilience and positive life changes, the more I convinced I became about the importance of spiritual intelligence to the psychological health of individuals and communities. But how does this relationship unfold? To answer this question, I began my study of spiritual intelligence by looking at the concept of *resilience*.

Many years ago I discovered the research on resilience that was pioneered by Norman Garmezy and his colleagues at the University of Minnesota. Resilience, as defined by Garmezy, a distinguished developmental psychologist, was the ability to respond to situations of extreme stress with extraordinary competence (Garmezy & Tellegen, 1984). Garmezy's interest in resilience derived from his observation that some children thrive despite living in conditions of severe adversity, such as parental alcoholism or mental illness; physical, sexual, and emotional abuse; or crippling socioeconomic and political situations. Other children were psychologically defeated by similar events. *Project Competence* was his 30-year quest to find out why.

Resilient people, according to many researchers (e.g., Anthony & Cohler, 1987; Dugan & Coles, 1989; Flach, 1988; Garmezy & Tellegen, 1984; Higgins, 1994), are intelligent, emotionally flexible, and willing to reach out for love and support from a wide variety of sources. They are more independent, sensitive, and curious than their less resilient peers, and more willing to rely on their own inner resources. They cultivate and cherish their sense of humor and are optimistic in the face of adversity; no matter how dire the circumstances in which they find themselves, they believe in their ability to exercise some measure of control over their lives. Because they are committed to living as fully as possible, they develop their talents and abilities, acquire a high degree of personal discipline, and are willing to fight to preserve their own souls.

Resilient people are also altruistic, introspective, and reflective. They strive for a coherent philosophy of life that bolsters their psychological health and helps them maintain their emotional vitality. They learn to turn to themselves for comfort and safety and to trust their own thoughts and beliefs rather than accept unquestioningly the ideas of those around them. They take time to recuperate from trauma and setbacks, and they savor both the process and progress of their lives. Resilient individuals are not superhuman, nor are they saints, but as Lois Murphy discovered, they "*want[ed]* to be resilient and actively mobilize[ed] and respond[ed] to anything and everything that [would] contribute to recovery" (1987, pp. 104-105; emphasis in original).

The concept of resilience struck a powerful personal chord when I first encountered it and seemed intuitively connected to my spiritual experiences. I remembered a former therapist asking me how I had managed to survive my parents' emotional abuse and complete rejection without becoming mentally ill or socio-pathic. Although I could never answer her question to her complete satisfaction, I knew that my spiritual awareness was intimately involved. The guiding spirits of my childhood, who taught me to tune into a higher reality in order to cope with my parents' cruelty and psychological immaturity, had kept me from suicide when I was 14-years-old by reminding me that there were answers to be found if I had the courage to ask the right questions. They led me through a series of dreams to a new life in Seattle and gave me clues at critical moments about where to look for work or financial aid in order to complete my education (Noble, 1994). During the spiritual event I described in the Prologue, they answered my most pressing questions, an encounter that crystallized my determination to be a psychologi-cally healthy human being. Would I have been as resilient without this awareness? The answer was unequivocally *no.*

Since becoming a psychologist 15 years ago, I have come to know many people who demonstrated an equally powerful commitment to their psychological growth. They also had to bring their resilience to bear on the brutalities and traumas of their lives, yet the qualities thus far identified with resilience did not sufficiently explain their fierce determination to bring psychological order out of overwhelming chaos. *Why* were they determined to be well? What role did spiritual intelligence play in this ongoing process? How did their spiritual experiences support their efforts to be healthier, more mature, and more humane than family or community members had been to them?

Advanced technologies like Magnetic Resonance Imaging and the Hubble Space Telescope have enabled scientists to see previously invisible aspects of the physical universe in extraordinary detail, but we lack similar devices with which to explore the intricacies of the spiritual realm. As noted in Chapter Two, instruments that assess spiritual experiences currently provide no gauge of spiritual intelligence. For that one must look to individuals' narrative histories and their understanding of how spiritual phenomena influenced their psychological development.

Andrew Weil observed that "the aim of scientific inquiry is not to reveal absolute truth but to discover more and more useful ways of thinking about phenomena" (1972, p. 10). Despite the difficulties inherent in gathering and interpreting data from retrospective case histories and self-reports, I felt that this approach would yield new and powerful ways to think about the role of spiritual intelligence in advancing psychological development.

Thus, I decided to conduct semi-structured interviews with nine adults and to ask them to reflect on the role that spirituality played and plays in their lives. Each interview took from 2 to 3 hours to complete, each was taperecorded and transcribed by me, and all were analyzed for content and themes individually and as a group. The questions I asked were open-ended and included the following:

- What were your most psychologically significant life experiences? What was life in your family like?
- What was/is your religious background and belief system?
- What does "spirituality" mean to you? What kinds of spiritual experiences have you had and when did you have them?
- How have these experiences affected your personality, relationships, vocational interests, psychological and physical health, values, goals, and life plans?
- Has it been a challenge to cope with the aftermath of your spiritual experience/s? In what way/s?
- What has been the most surprising thing to you about your spiritual experiences? What have you learned?
- How important is spirituality in your life?
- What are you doing with your life now, and why?

My informants included five women and four men. Two were clients, two were colleagues, four were individuals referred to me by colleagues who knew about my work, and one was an acquaintance who had read one of my books. All their names have been changed to assure confidentiality. Participants were between the ages of 25 and 50. Their ethnic backgrounds included African American, Caucasian, Chicano/Native American, Latino Caribbean, and Southeast Asian. All were current or former practitioners of established religions, including various branches of Buddhism, Christianity, Islam, and Judaism. The cohort included a sociologist, a physician, a psychologist, a computer programmer, a homemaker/sculptor, a hair designer, a graduate student, a teacher, and an advertising salesperson. Three participants were gay or lesbian. Several suffered from physical illnesses and disabilities: one person was struggling to recover from alcoholism, one was HIV positive, one had chronic fatigue syndrome, and one had severe fibromyalgia. Three respondents were also recovering from posttraumatic stress syndrome, and several had struggled with depression.

In choosing people to interview I was looking for a certain combination of qualities and traits. Because I wanted informants who would be considered resilient by the most rigorous standards, I carefully chose people who were committed, compassionate, and psychologically alive, and who had experienced enough trauma that they could easily have turned out differently. I wanted people who were actively working on their emotional and psychological health, and who were giving back to their communities in ways they thought were meaningful. I wanted people who represented a wide variety of ethnic, racial, occupational, and religious backgrounds; who had a diversity of spiritual experiences; and who were neither fundamental nor fanatical in their orientation to the spiritual realm. No one who took part in this study claimed to be a "guru," no one was known for having extraordinary talent in the supernatural realm, and no one earned a living giving psychic or spiritual advice.

As their stories unfold, some readers might wonder whether participants' experiences are "spiritual" or "psychological" in nature and origin. Unfortunately, words both elucidate and confound our understanding of complex phenomena. Conventional usage designates certain experiences, such as dreams and intuition, as *psychological* events; others, like telepathy or clairvoyance, are commonly called *psychic* or *paranormal.* Mystical and transcendent experiences are usually labeled *spiritual.* I believe that all such distinctions are purely arbitrary and ultimately meaningless.

There is no professional or lay agreement about where the psychological ends and the spiritual begins. Although the word *psychology* derives from ancient Greek and means the study of the psyche or the soul, students would be hard-pressed to find a modern psychology course in most secular educational institutions that takes seriously the idea of a soul. As noted in Chapter Two, scientists who believe that psychological and spiritual events are biologically based dominate contemporary psychology. Are spiritual experiences the result of electrical or biochemical activity in different parts of the brain, or do they reflect the existence of nonphysical realities that are largely imperceptible to our physical senses? Does consciousness precede or originate in the brain? What is consciousness? These are mysteries that investigators in the emerging field of consciousness studies are beginning to address, but their solution lies many years in the future. Psychology is a young discipline, barely a century old, and must progress further before the self can be examined as minutely as the cell. After all, most physicians denied the reality of bacteria and viruses before the invention of the microscope, and without cyclotrons, physicists would be unaware of leptons and quarks. Although I wish that I could answer these questions definitively, they are open-ended and readers must come to their own conclusions.

Some of the stories that follow are subtle; others are sobering. Some are familiar and others are esoteric. Yet each offers integral insights into the extraordinary puzzle we call the Self, and each reminds us "not only that the world is a stranger place than we could otherwise suppose, but also how difficult it is to arrive at any definite conclusions about it" (Beloff, 1975, p. 11).

CHAPTER FOUR

Spiritual Awakenings

It is a shocking thing to know so much about oneself
in such a little time.
  —James T. Lester (1983)

Three months before her 10-month-old son was killed in an automobile accident, Megan had an experience that seemed, in retrospect, to be a portent. Megan is a stone sculptor, a wife, and a mother; she told me this story while we were sitting in her garden next to a boulder on which she had carved an intricate design. "I used to have two little Indian RingNecked parrots that I had raised from tiny babies. They had apparently escaped from a breeder, naturalized, and nested in an old oak tree. One day the babies got knocked out of the tree. Apparently when it's a very dry season, the mother will stagger the hatching of the eggs. One of the babies had its feathers and I found it sitting on a little fence when I went down to get the mail; then my dog discovered another one at the foot of the tree. That one didn't even have its pin feathers yet, and it had a broken leg. I brought them home and called several people for advice, all of whom told me they'd never survive. So I tried to imagine what their mother would do. I knew they were omnivorous so I gathered seeds and bugs and started feeding them. I built a cage and set it out on our deck next to an oak tree, and then the adult birds discovered that their babies were there. I turned the cage so the door was up and the adults would take turns feeding the babies. Those birds meant everything to me at the time. Everything else was put aside. I had them for about eleven years."

"One day in the springtime I took them outside. By that time I knew I had a male and a female, and they were getting a bit amorous. The female had laid a couple of eggs so I was fiddling around with the cage when suddenly the male flew out. Unfortunately, being a caged bird, he couldn't fly very well. I knew he wouldn't fly far, but he couldn't fly away from the cat who got to him before I could. My daughter was five at the time, my son about 8 months old, and my husband was away. I remember holding that little bird, saying out loud, 'my baby, my little boy.' I remember actually catching myself saying these things and hoping nobody heard me. Well, maybe it's pretty crazy but I feel like that was a premonition because of what happened a few months later."

"One of my sisters and my children and I were coming back from California where we had been visiting relatives. It was my birthday and we were driving a Volkswagen bus over the summit of a mountain pass. It was early evening and my son was getting tired of sitting in his car seat. My sister had just taken him out of it because he was fussy, and she knew that I had to concentrate on driving that treacherous pass. Suddenly a big truck came out of the blue, lost its breaks, and rear-ended us. When my sister was thrown forward my son was thrown out the window. And the things I said to my little parrot were the same things I found myself saying when I was running up the road looking for him. I've thought back to that so many times. Just before the accident I was agitated and irritable in a way that I didn't understand. I now feel quite certain that something was trying to get through to me and I just didn't get it . . ."

"Now this is the thing that I've had the hardest time understanding. I *know* that I went with my son when he died. I remember feeling the impact but I couldn't have told you what hit us. And then I remember soaring out over the precipice. We were all together, my sister and my children, and it was inexpressibly calm, warm, light, and peaceful. I remember thinking, 'Well, we're all together.' Funny little things that we had been taught in safety education were running though my mind, like 'just relax and go with it.' I was certain that in the end we would wind up in the bottom of the ravine, but I had no sense of fighting what was happening. At one point I remember thinking, "So this is what it's like to die.'"

"When I came to, my sister, my daughter, and I were lying on the road and the car was on its side. I don't know where my son was. I remember running up the road looking for him. There were concrete dividers down the center, and I got up on them, screaming, 'Where's my baby, where's my baby?' I saw something on the road and I ran toward it, but a man was walking down the road and he got to me just before I got to that something. He held me back and said, 'You don't want to see that baby, that baby's in heaven now.' And then he took me under his arm and walked me to my car."

Megan told me this story several years after her son had been killed in that tragic accident. The shock and its emotional aftermath would never fully fade, but she and her family had slowly come to terms with his death, and they found ways to integrate the experience and his memory into their lives. What Megan could not resolve, however, was the experience of accompanying her son to the threshold of death and watching him cross over, an experience that left as much confusion as serenity in its wake. To be sure, it had comforted and reassured her and helped her to heal, but it also unlocked inner depths of which she had been completely unaware and raised questions for which nothing in her past had prepared her.

Megan was the seventh child of Scots-Irish parents, the adored and rambunctious baby of the family. Her father was a scientist, her mother a housewife; both were active, intellectual, and pillars of their community. Neither was religious and they never went to church, so Megan's introduction to religion was sporadic and minimal. When she was about 5-years-old, her older sisters tried to enroll her in a Methodist Sunday School but once there she always ran away; she didn't like the atmosphere or the experience, and eventually her sisters gave up.

The only childhood spiritual experience she remembers occurred when she was 8, shortly after her family moved into a new home. "My parents bought an unbelievable adobe house that had been built by two remarkable women whom we all met. They had made the bricks themselves. They were so happy that a family was going to be living there. The house was huge, about 13,000 square feet. It was really designed to be a school or a monastery, but the women wanted it to be for a family. They were women with dreams! They believed that world peace would come through the youth of the world, so they built the house not only as their home but as a publishing house for a magazine called *World Youth*. The house had a lot of soul and my parents always used to speak of 'the ghost of good fellowship' or 'the spirit of the house,' which was very good energy."

"Each of the women had her own suite of rooms," Megan continued. "Carolyn had a sitting room with a fireplace, a bedroom, and a bathroom; Maude had the same kind of set-up. I lived in what would have been Carolyn's suite with one of my sisters. We had twin beds. After they sold the house the ladies packed everything up because their dream was to travel and end up in Ireland, where one owned some property. They had travelled all over the world before and wanted to do that again."

"I remember one night after they had taken off and we had settled into the house. I was asleep but woke up when I heard the back door open. All the doors had handmade latches which made a special sound when they opened. I heard the latch going up and then footsteps coming in and down a little hallway. All of a sudden I could see a figure standing right outside the closed doorway to my bedroom! Then the figure came through the door and into the room, and just as it was leaning over and starting to touch the corner of my bed, I lost it. I screamed or something, my sister turned on the lights, and it was gone. But the next day we received a telegram from Maude in Switzerland who said that Carolyn had passed away in the night. We figured the time difference and realized that the figure I saw was Carolyn. Her spirit had come back. I can still recall how she was dressed. A few days later we found a hat in the garden that Carolyn used to wear and she was wearing it that night. Surprisingly, my parents both acknowledged that experience as more than just a child having a funny dream. When we got the telegram and put two and two together, it all fit. So I felt that whatever that experience had been was validated for me. It wasn't rejected as some childhood fantasy."

Megan's only other introduction to religion came when she was student teaching in a British Catholic school and able to observe her students performing and participating in a weekly Mass. She loved the ritual, which was moving and mysterious, but the religion itself left her cold, and her interest waned after she completed her teaching apprenticeship. Thus, when Megan escorted her son to the vestibule of death, she had no context into which to place the experience. It wasn't until she read about my spiritual experiences in an earlier book (Noble, 1994) that she began to understand the psychospiritual territory into which she had been thrust.

****

Susan called me several years ago in a state of deep distress. She is a brilliant physician, a former dancer, and an avid devotee of the arts who is extraordinarily moved by aesthetic and musical experiences. Susan had spent years working on her psychological health, but now she needed a therapist who could help her understand her spiritual experiences and their sequellae.

Susan's experience of family life can only be characterized as terrifying. Having tried unsuccessfully to give birth to a child, her Sicilian mother and German father finally decided to adopt a blond-haired, blue-eyed boy. Eleven months later Susan was born, but to parents who no longer wanted her. Her dark Italian appearance, keen intelligence, and high level of energy intensified her mother's ambivalence and made her the target of her father's uncontrollable rage. Susan never understood the roots of their rejection, but the effects would haunt her for years. She was physically and sexually abused by her father and shunned by her mother in favor of her brother, who in turn made Susan the object of his cruelty and deceit.

Susan's mother was raised in Sicily as a Roman Catholic, but she became virulently anti-religious after she was molested by a local priest at the age of 13. After her marriage, however, she acquiesced to her husband's demand that the family regularly attend church services. Susan's father, a career military officer, was a strict but generic Protestant for whom outer form was more important than inner substance. Because of his career the family moved frequently, attending whatever church was geographically closest to them. Although she had always been intrigued with spirituality, Susan hated going to church. Many elements of Christianity made no sense to her, and biblical misogyny and the hypocrisy of her parents' private behavior especially repelled her. Moreover, the refusal of successive ministers to answer difficult questions, especially those concerning evolution and creation, and their admonition to take things "on faith," troubled her deeply. One day when she was 12, Susan decided she would no longer attend church, a decision that caused an uproar in her family. "I got beaten several times for this," she said. "It never made sense to me to be beaten over church. In fact, it seemed pretty crazy but my father was insistent. Finally he gave in, and amazingly enough my mother stopped going as well. She had never wanted to go because she hated church and thought religion was 'ridiculous,' but she was unwilling to stand up to him. So unbeknownst to me, I did it for her."

Susan had a voracious appetite for learning and threw herself into a wide range of studies and activities. She married after she completed her undergraduate degree, but her husband's psychological instability and physical violence led to their divorce a few years later. Subsequently, Susan decided to pursue her love of science and was accepted into medical school where she found that her intuition occasionally allowed her to make uncanny diagnoses. She first became aware of this ability when she was a medical student rotating through various hospital wards. "At patients' bedsides I would suddenly sense things. It's more a kinesthetic kind of knowing. I don't know where the information came from but it drove the other doctors crazy. I had to be very careful. If I said, 'This person has a tumor in his abdomen,' they'd look at me and say 'Right.' But I would know and generally I'd be proven right. Sometimes the proof would take several weeks, but when I had that knowing, it was truth. I remember once looking at a child who had a germ tumor of the ovary. Everybody said she had a kidney tumor but I said no, this is a teratoma. I didn't even know what a teratoma was but I knew she had one. The experience of making a diagnosis I had no right to make happened at least a dozen times, and it was spooky because I didn't know what was going on and neither did anyone else."

During her last two years of training Susan suddenly developed puzzling neurological symptoms and extreme fatigue, ailments that were initially misdiagnosed as psychosomatic, a combination of depression and stress. Through an enormous effort of will Susan completed medical school, but shortly after she graduated her symptoms intensified. "When they got into my hands I knew I wasn't crazy. I had been studying dance and trying to rehabilitate my body because something was wrong and nobody could figure it out; then suddenly I was unable to walk. I became terribly weak and completely bedridden for long periods of time. Sometimes I was only able to move for a few minutes each day. There were times when I would have to tie up my arms because they were too weak to hold at my sides. I felt very confused and I was very frightened. It was pretty bad." Her anxiety was exacerbated by the fact that her parents refused to help or support her in any way, her closest friends had taken residencies in other states, and she was left virtually alone.

Susan consulted a variety of specialists and was told she had multiple sclerosis, a diagnosis that would also prove false when, many years later, her quest for a cure finally disclosed a neck fracture and spinal cord compression sustained during a childhood gymnastics accident. At the time the MS diagnosis was made, however, "the doctor told me there was nothing he could do for me and that I had to figure out how to live in a wheelchair. That's when I turned on all the juices and started experimenting with macrobiotics and new age healing practices. I also did a lot of questioning. Why is this happening? What is the meaning of suffering? Why me, God? I couldn't do much so I had a lot of time to think."

"Several things came together at that point. My dance teacher was very spiritual and steered me in the direction of meditation. I ended up reading a lot of books about it, especially by Steven Levine. I had studied relaxation techniques in the early 1970s so I started doing them again. Then I started sitting Zazen, crossed leg meditation, although I was so weak I could only do it for a few minutes at a time. I would do various forms of meditation, basically as a way of relaxing and controlling my fear because I was terrified and I needed to get my mind under control. Sometimes I would meditate for an hour or two a day, using breath awareness and the mantra *om mane padme hum*.

"Then, one night, about ten years ago, I had a very powerful experience. I was meditating and suddenly I had an intense sensation of a Buddha in front of me. I had studied enough Asian art to recognize various Buddhas and their styles, and this one was a medicine Buddha. It had a greenish caste and looked like a wooden Buddha with a bronze covering on it. I was very deep in meditation at that point, and it stayed there when I focused my awareness on it. It seemed almost solid but I realized it was more of a mental image. The Buddha had a little container in one hand and a lotus in the other, and I heard myself say, 'Oh, the lotus!' Then I realized that the mantra, om mane padme hum, means the jewel inside of the lotus. I looked in the lotus, and there was a rose colored crystal at its center. Suddenly the whole Buddha turned and became me at exactly the moment when I thought the mantra. I felt a really strong sensation of energy at the base of my spine that was like a white column that came up and formed a sort of halo around my head, and then I just disappeared. I was a little frightened, but I stayed with the mantra, which was very comforting."

"Then I realized that I had awareness but nothing else and no body. The place that I went to was formless and timeless, and there was also a sense of omnipotence and omniscience. I was surrounded by all-knowing and all-being, and I felt a sense of other consciousnesses or awarenesses with me. Everything was the same kind of energy but more solid, like ice cubes—compact areas of awareness that seemed to comprise the individuals. But that isn't really accurate because I had no sense of individuality. Everybody knew everything and there was no separateness. It was very blissful. I assumed that this was what was meant by the oneness and eternity of being."

"I came back into my body after an indeterminate time, and I immediately wondered, 'What was that?' I knew it was real. It was not a psychotic experience. It was not some kind of dream. It was one of the most real experiences I ever had, but I hadn't a clue as to what had happened to me. That was the jet propulsion that got me on the path to read and ask questions. It initiated an amazing search for information. Most of what I subsequently learned had to do with ideas of chakras, energies, spiritual emergencies, and kundalini experiences. I had somehow stumbled into a great event that many people try for 20 or 30 years to experience, and I did it in a few months. Very few people in my meditation circle would talk with me about it, and some told me I couldn't have had that experience because it was only for adepts or grand masters, not for ordinary people like me. But some spiritual advisers said it probably occurred through a combination of the intense concentration I had learned in medical school, plus an open heart and a desire to do good. That combination, with a little meditation on top, blew my whole life apart."

****

Tomas was raised on a top-secret American military installation, the first born son of "Russian, Hungarian, Austrian, Polish, Jewish parents" who were ambitious, intellectual, and extremely achievement-oriented. His father was a renowned physicist who during Tomas' childhood was engaged in highly classified research; his mother authored several books, and his siblings grew up to be doctors and lawyers. "I'm fond of saying I'm the least achieving member of my family," Tomas laughed. "Actually, there's something I like about that." Now in his mid-40s, Tomas is playful, introspective, compassionate, and deeply committed to social and ecological activism, qualities that he reports are relatively recent developments.

Tomas was a highly sensitive boy who felt completely out of place both at home and on the military base. His father was domineering, judgmental, and psychologically abusive; his mother was emotionally absent and offered no protection from his father's verbal assaults. His elementary school and community seemed to him to have been bleached of everything that was beautiful or alive. As a result, Tomas became quiet and withdrawn, except for a brief period in the second grade when he acted out his anger and aggression toward other children. When that period passed, however, Tomas settled into being "a highly rational, controlled, and controlling child who hated flowers and socks," and who rejected anything that wasn't logical and mechanical. Like his father, Tomas possessed a strong aptitude for science and mathematics, proclivities that became more pronounced as he grew older. His hatred of his father, however, made him reject those qualities in himself, and he spent years struggling against his own nature. Finally, after dropping out of three different colleges and spending several years attempting to major in art, Tomas could no longer tolerate the terrible tension of trying to be what he clearly was not. One day he abruptly changed his major to physics, and then went on to enjoy successful academic and professional careers. For 15 years he worked successively as a computer programmer, a computer manager, a business planner, and a marketing representative for an electronics company, and then took what was supposed to have been a two-week vacation in Thailand. Six months later, however, he was still in Asia, unable to abide the thought of returning to his former life but unsure about what to do next.

Although ethnically Jewish, no one in Tomas' family practiced Judaism or was interested in spirituality, and neither was he. "I identify as a Jew but I don't know how to say exactly what that means," Tomas said. "I wouldn't say I'm an atheist because to me that means that it's possible to believe in God, an afterlife, or an immortal soul, and I don't." Thus, the crystallizing experience that engulfed him in his mid-30s came as a complete surprise. Extremely articulate as a rule, Tomas fell silent as he sought the words to describe this event. "This is the thing about which I feel enormously defensive," he said. "The reason is that I'm so ready for someone to say that my spiritual experiences aren't *real* spiritual experiences, or that they don't count, or aren't real enough, and I'm absolutely convinced that they are."

"The first time I had this experience I had taken LSD. All I wanted to do was to lie down and be quiet in a quiet place, and relax my body, my breathing, my thinking, and then my thoughts. For some reason LSD magnified my concentration and enabled me to sense what I now call a 'threshold' place. I hesitate about whether to say a new place because it didn't feel new. It felt as if I had come for the first time to a place that had always been there. I describe it as a physical place but it's not a physical place; it doesn't feel physical, but I don't know how to talk about it other than to make it sound as if it is. Some of its qualities are a largeness, an emptiness of words, and a tremendous feeling of the falling away of everything that is superficial and irrelevant, everything that is worshiped as the centerpiece of life in this culture. And what also seemed to fall away were all the details and the unimportant parts of myself, and all my thoughts which kept me separate from myself. And then suddenly I was at the center of myself, and I saw that I was on the threshold of an incredibly beautiful place. . . ." Tomas shook his head in frustration. "Words are hard because whatever this place is, it's more important than beautiful, it's absolutely *right*. Wherever I was, I had no physical or emotional needs. I'm very often an insecure person, and I need a lot of approval and reassurance from people, so to be in this place and to know I am *enough* is indescribable. The whole experience felt tremendously stabilizing and nurturing. It gave me a sense of a foundation to stand on and opened up parts of myself I never knew existed."

****

Valerie's memories of her early childhood are filled with light, laughter, and flights of imagination shared with her mother. The eldest of three children, she was the adored and adoring daughter of intellectual, professional, and affluent parents who spent much of their free time hiking, travelling, and playing with their young family. Valerie remembered that a sentient blue light used to visit her repeatedly when she was a young girl. "Actually, it was turquoise, almost white blue and very brilliant, more of a light than a color. When it would come around me I would say, 'Oh my friend Blue is here.' It really felt like a friend. I didn't know what it was, but I knew it was real and it was very comforting. I don't remember that it would come at any particular crisis; it came more 'out of the blue' so to speak," she laughed. "After I turned 12 or so it didn't come any more. I'm not sure why except that I was aware that other people didn't seem to have color friends."

Valerie looked happy when she told me this story, but as she began to remember her adolescence her eyes clouded, and her countenance foretold the subsequent destruction of her family's life and her desperate struggle to stay emotionally well. By the time she turned 14, Valerie's father had succumbed to workaholism and he withdrew from the family. Her mother became depressed and alcoholic, and her parents soon divorced. As the eldest child, Valerie was unwillingly thrust into a parental role, which her younger siblings desperately needed but deeply resented and for which she was completely unprepared. The result was a descent into psychological hell from which she would not emerge for years.

Valerie coped with her new circumstances as best she could, but her unmet emotional needs made her vulnerable to intimate relationships before she was psychologically ready for them. She also began to drink, a habit that would lead to her own alcoholism many years later. The only bright spot in Valerie's life was high school, where she was nurtured by her teachers and given the structure she needed to shine socially, intellectually, and athletically. After she graduated, Valerie entered college, and though she was unfocused she continued to excel until the day she was viciously assaulted by a man she had been dating for some months.

Several factors may have triggered this attack—her boyfriend's depression and emotional dependency, her own emotional vulnerability, his use of cocaine, or her decision to break up with him—but they are a jumble of darkness and confusion in her mind. What is clear is that the explosion, when it came, was almost lethal. As a male friend of theirs stood by and watched, Valerie was beaten and kicked into unconsciousness; when she came to she discovered that the men were gone, and somehow she managed to get herself home. Once there she collapsed and was rushed to the hospital and into emergency surgery. In addition to bruises and a concussion, Valerie's spleen had been ruptured and over half her body's blood was lost through internal bleeding, leaving her perilously close to death. Although her body made a rapid recovery and within a month she was able to walk and get around, her psyche had been shattered, along with her faith in the world's goodness to which she had clung so tenaciously throughout her adolescence. "The world I had lived in no longer made sense," Valerie said. "I couldn't understand or integrate the emotional wound, the sense of violation, of almost losing my life for no good reason, and the collapse of my belief in the just ordering of the world. So I ran away."

Valerie fled to California and landed in Berkeley, where she had vague thoughts about attending the university. But this idea never materialized. Instead, she became a nomad, living by her wits from one day to the next, staying on the streets or in someone's home, trusting her survival to her instincts. At one point all her identification documents were stolen, an act that stripped her of any sense of identity and seemed somehow inevitable. Valerie drank, partied, and danced in and out of dangerous situations, but she always managed to escape unharmed. Many months later, however, a succession of three powerful dreams convinced her that it was time to put her self and her life back together.

"The first was an earthquake dream. Obviously, living as I was I was literally on shaky ground, but in my dream I was in an earthquake and I kept trying to wake up. I would think I was awake but then realize I was still in a dream. That had never happened to me before, waking from one dream only to find myself in another. When I finally did wake up I was in a cold sweat and shaking. That was an incredibly jarring experience."

"The next night I dreamt that I was at a party with a lot of people I knew, club owners and movers and shakers, and I started to realize that something was very wrong. I was amusing to them, but I felt a cold, calculating sense of being preyed upon. I felt that I *was* prey. I woke up thinking, 'Hmm . . . these people don't have my best interests at heart. Isn't that a revelation?'"

"The third night I had the most powerful and transformative experience that I've ever had. I dreamt I was in a warehouse, a dance club like many of the places I frequented in my waking life, only much bigger. It was dark and everyone was dancing to funky music. I noticed that I didn't have any feet and was floating up and down. I thought that it was awfully odd that I was floating and no one was willing or able to acknowledge that this was a little unusual. I went to the ladies' room and had a real unsafe feeling, and then I realized that I was in the party from hell. So I walked out, and the next thing I knew I was on a bus."

"Once on the bus I felt very comfortable. There were people around and a tour guide standing at the front. I looked at him and he handed me a brochure that said 'A Ticket to Heaven.' When the bus stopped I got out at a huge complex. There was brilliant white light all around and I started running down this corridor. There was a little spirit who seemed like he couldn't keep up with me, who kept saying, 'Wait a minute, hold on!', but I had to get where I was going. I finally arrived at an empty theater that was fairly austere, simple, and white. I went along the back row and suddenly began to sing the song of myself."

Valerie started to cry softly and paused to collect herself before she continued. "All of a sudden musicians started gathering on the stage and people started coming in and I felt 'Uh oh, I can't do this right, I'm going to mess up.' I stopped singing even though I knew I was in a very safe, very wonderful place. As soon as I stopped I heard my name being called, but I just said, 'I can't do this right.' So I ran out and then I was back in the party in hell. And I looked around and thought, 'What these people need is love.' I tried with all my strength to emanate love to the beings dancing there, and one by one they turned into multicolored particles and disappeared, until the room was virtually empty. Then I walked out and woke up. And I thought, 'Hmm . . . over there they're working on a symphony and I'm invited and I have a part to sing, but I was too afraid.' I think there is a party in hell going on and I've been there, done that. But I also know there's a symphony. That realization and that experience got me off the streets."

Valerie made an appointment to see me shortly after she returned from her sojourn in California. She was living with family members and adjusting to being home but barely holding her body and soul together. The assault by her boyfriend and its catastrophic aftermath had triggered the eruption of many unresolved childhood traumas and resulted in complex posttraumatic stress syndrome. Valerie's rage toward God, her feelings of betrayal and abandonment by her family, and her confusion and despair were spiraling out of control and leading her deeper into the darkness of alcoholism. Yet, at the same time she knew that her powerful dreams had saved her life and had begun to transform her in some inexplicable way. Somehow the intervention of the spiritual realm had not only kept her alive but galvanized her decision to heal and prevail. What had happened and what this meant was the point of our departure.

****

Alex grew up in a close and loving family on the East Coast, the son of Latino Caribbean parents who emigrated to the United States so that his father could complete his medical training. Alex is imaginative and artistic, and as a child he loved to paint, draw, and illustrate stories he had written. Although his light brown complexion made it difficult for him to feel at home within the Anglo and African American groups that dominated his schools, his gregarious personality won him acceptance and friends. Unfortunately, as he grew into adolescence, it also won him a reputation for drinking, partying, and "being burnt." Despite his intelligence and creativity, Alex was not particularly motivated, and he had no sense of a calling beyond "calling my friend for the next party." He did, however, graduate from high school and college and earn a certificate to teach.

Alex worked as a substitute teacher for a year, an experience that was difficult and not very rewarding. As a result, he decided to apply to a Fine Arts graduate program on the West Coast in the hope that it would galvanize his creative energies and re-engage him in the process of writing and illustrating his stories and poems. Initially the move seemed promising, but several months after arriving in Seattle, his emotions went into a nose-dive. The college friends with whom Alex was sharing an apartment turned out to be incompatible, and he felt unwelcome in his home. In addition, he had not expected the competition and criticism that defines the climate in graduate school and, as a result, his creativity was suppressed rather than released. When he realized that the life he expected to find in Seattle was failing to materialize, Alex became severely depressed, a condition that lasted for almost a year and which resolved itself in a most unexpected manner.

"During this period I was thinking all the time. For the first time I was wondering about the meaning of life and other big issues and trying to think my way to the answers, but it wasn't working and I was just becoming more depressed. One night I went to a lecture by a former Hindu priest who had converted to Christianity and wrote a book about the process. One of the things he said was, basically, turn your mind to Jesus and he'll help you out. The speaker had a certain charm about him so later, when I was walking home, I stopped and said, 'OK, I'm here, let me know. Contact me. Comfort me.' I waited for awhile under a tree but nothing happened, and I went home, still bummed out."

"When I got home some guys I knew were going out to a nearby bar so I went along. We were sitting in the bar when all of a sudden I felt some kind of energy flood into my head. I saw one guy laughing and I suddenly had a strong impression that *love* was the whole reason for everything. And in this vision I saw a little black stream in space and I knew it was possible to jump

over that to other realms. It was really weird. I felt kind of restless so I left the bar and walked over to a pool hall, which is
where things really got otherworldly. I saw this really big Biker
who was smiling; he seemed friendly and well intentioned, and I
saw—not with my real eye but with something like an eye in my
chest—an incredible light coming out of him. It wasn't really an
aura, but rather rays of pure light coming not from his face but
from some other realm *behind* him. I've never seen a light like
this before or since. It was amber-orange-gold, more like a laser
than an ordinary light. This light was coming out from him, from
me, from my other friend, and then I realized that it was coming
out of everyone. After awhile I went home and went to sleep,
thinking that maybe it was just my imagination. But when I woke
up the next day I discovered that I really believed that experience
had happened and that there were agents out there who would
help us. I felt there was a personal dimension to the universe I
had never sensed before."

"A few days later some guys in my neighborhood encouraged me to go to church with them; they said that there were lots
of different cultures there and that it was really neat. Well I went,
but I found it to be very fear-based and fundamentalist, which
was completely unlike the beautiful and loving connection I had
felt with the universe in my experience, and I never went again. I
did go to a class on the near-death experience, though, and that
was good for me because as I listened to people talk about otherworldly guidance it sort of blew the lid off my reasoning process.
Listening to other people's stories about their spiritual experiences made it easier for me to accept the unusual."

"Well, a few weeks later I went to a rock concert. It was
really jammed; there was an avalanche of bodies pressing against
the security fences, trying to break them down, and I felt really
disturbed. There were so many people getting hurt, and it seemed
like the band was really encouraging the darker energies, the
panic and the drunkenness of the crowd. I was dancing and trying to create a little positive energy around me, and all of a sudden I felt as though I had entered a wonderful emotional realm
that was deeper and unlike anything I ever felt before. I felt that I
understood what Alan Watts was talking about when he said
we're all the same being playing the same game. The earth, the
trees, the wind, friends, we're all beautiful and on some level we

all know who we are. I felt an incredible organic unity to the universe, that it was made up of limitless forms that were all the same thing. But the feelings were so intense that I suddenly felt very anxious and unsafe, so I left the concert and went outside and tried to relax by concentrating on feeling the grass and the breeze. There were some young kids standing there, about 14-years-old, and they seemed to want to talk with me. I think I told them I was freaking out a little, and they said they knew and they had come to find me and help me calm down. 'It's like wolves,' they said. 'Wolves can always sense when somebody in the tribe is in trouble and they come and help them.' Suddenly it was like an intuitive switch got turned on in my mind. That was when I *knew* that we, this whole earth, are part of the fabric of paradise. We're all the same fabric. Now is the time to enjoy, to create, to express, to dance, to feel. You know, my depression dropped away and since then it has never come back. I was energized for a long time, and I felt a real affective change in myself, a certain buoyancy I hadn't felt since I was a kid. This whole experience set me back on track."

****

Maya is a thoughtful, soft-spoken graduate student with an intensely active mind and an equally inquisitive soul. She also has one of the more difficult combinations of life challenges. Maya and her twin sister were born in Germany but raised in the Midwest, where her father was a university professor and her mother completed her doctoral degree in sociology. The town in which they lived was a "very white, very blonde" environment, in which Maya felt completely out of place. "My mom's Anglo, and my dad's a mixture of Anglo, Mexican, and Native American," she confided. "He always claims that he's white and that we're white, but I was very confused ethnically as a kid. If you look at family photographs, my mom is white, my dad isn't, and my sister and I are shaded right in between. When I started growing up, boys would walk up to me and say 'Do you speak English?' I looked weird because I had jet-black hair and reddish-brown skin. It wasn't until I left home and went away to college that I began to be comfortable with my mixed race heritage."

Growing up was difficult for Maya beyond divergence from the community's ethnic norm. Because she and her sister were very bright, their parents expected them to be little adults and to take care of each other. "Both my parents taught and were hardly ever home, so we were responsible for each other," Maya said. "My dad recently coined the phrase *spectator parenting*, which I think is a good description of what they did. It means that you don't want to get too involved in raising children; you could spectate and be proud from a distance. That always struck me as an excuse for not taking responsibility for being an adult." Moreover, her parents' relationship was distant and unstable, and they expended little energy on their daughters' emotional needs. When her sister's ex-boyfriend raped Maya and her sister during their senior year of high school, their parents' response was characteristically cold. "They gave us no resources or assistance to deal with sexual assault," Maya sighed. "Two years later I came out as a lesbian. I had been scared about it for a long time and in denial. Of course, they were no help with that either."

Physical disability contributed yet another element to the emotional rapids Maya was forced to navigate. She and her sister both suffer from fibromyalgia, a painful and chronic musculoskeletal condition that began in their adolescence. "My sister showed signs when she was 14," Maya said, "but it took a long time to get her diagnosed and many people thought she was crazy. She was in incredible pain and I was responsible for her care, but I had no power so it was a very difficult situation to be in. And then when I was 18 I got the disease too. We both went from being dancers to being in wheelchairs. My arms and legs spasmed so badly that I would fall down. I'm better now, but my sister is still in and out of a chair."

When Maya was a senior in high school, one of her friends was suddenly stricken with a rare and paralyzing disease for which she was hospitalized in an Intensive Care Unit for several months. "All she could do was blink her eyes and we would spell out words," Maya recalled. "The awful thing about this disease was that even though she was paralyzed, she was in total pain. The medics and I would try to communicate with her about where she was feeling pain so we could relieve it, but she was unable to talk. I discovered that I could suddenly know where she hurt and I would tell the medics, 'It's her left leg or right arm or right hand.' Usually it would be such a tense situation that they wouldn't question me. Sometimes they would look at me funny, wondering what I heard that they didn't, and I would just say, 'Do something about it.' I would take their attention away from how I got that information. I always wondered if later, when she could talk, she would ask me about that, but she never did. I was actually relieved because I couldn't explain it. I believe it was the urgency of her situation that made me receptive to that kind of information, and I figured I would find a way later to explain it if I needed to."

When Maya graduated from high school she chose to attend college as far away from home as possible, but once there she fell apart, physically and emotionally. She had no one to care for her as she had cared for her sister or her friend, and the university administration was not at all supportive. "Some university officials even made me sign a contract to the effect that no one would assist me or carry my meals even though the meal tray was too heavy for me. I think they were scared about liability, and at one point they told me I would have to go home until I could act like everybody else. This was in 1986; they wouldn't say that anymore but they said it then." One day Maya's despair overwhelmed her, and she made a serious attempt to kill herself by cutting her wrists and forearms. Remarkably, she didn't die, but she was left with scars that she was told she would have for the rest of her life. "I was just devastated when I realized they wouldn't go away," she recalled with tears in her eyes. "I was having so much conflict about the scars in both my public and private life, and I felt so branded that I wore long sleeves all the time."

The following Thanksgiving Maya decided to stay home by herself and be "spiritual." "Thanksgiving has a lot of meaning for me because of my Native background," she said. "I didn't have anything in mind, really, except making a pumpkin pie, cleaning my room, and just being with myself. I collect boxes of matches, and as I was straightening things up I found a blank one and decided to write something on it. Without thinking I wrote *marked for life*. As Maya stared at these words she suddenly realized that she was talking about the scars left from her suicide attempt. I realized that what I meant was that I was marked *for* life. I was *for* life as opposed to death, and my scars were meant to remind me that my ultimate choice is to live. So when people asked me later how my 'spiritual Thanksgiving' was, I said, 'very spiritual, thank you.' You know, when I told people about wanting to have a spiritual experience I didn't really expect anything to happen or to have any kind of revelation. I was just saying it. And then it happened."

****

Tony is a charismatic and energetic man in his mid-40s, the fourth child of a French Canadian-Canadian Indian father and a Pennsylvania Dutch mother. When he was 8, Tony had an extraordinary experience that helped him to keep his wits about him when his mother was losing hers. "My mother had an oscillating machine which she kept in her closet," Tony said. "It was supposedly one of those miracle things that took stress out of your feet. My parents were always fighting, every single day. I hated the sound of their fights so once I went into her bedroom, which was totally off-limits, shut the door, plugged in the oscillator, and laid my face in the water. I'm surprised I still have my vision now. Suddenly these little beings came bouncing all around me and talked to me, telling me that everything was going to be okay. They moved real fast, and I went into what I suspect was a different reality. I now know they were my spirit guides, but I didn't know that as a child. After that first time I must have used that oscillator hundreds of times to help me go where I needed to go. It became an automatic reflex. I wanted to stay in that other realm forever. I did not want to come back. Even though I was able to function and deal with the family, there was so much anxiety around. It was not a healthy environment for a child to develop in." Tony looked away wistfully. "I always hoped that Tinkerbell would appear because I loved the Peter Pan story," he laughed, "but she never did."

"Well, one time my mother caught me, and she was just furious. Not only did she think I would ruin my eyes, but I was using something of hers and I was in her room without permission, which was completely taboo. She started slapping me and screaming, and I remember sticking my head back in the closet to connect with the little beings. For some reason, that particular experience allowed me to bind together my physical, mental, and spiritual energies to perceive these little entities. They said 'Relax, be calm, you're going to be OK.' After that I was able to find them whenever I was being beaten or punished. I remember once I was forced to kneel on the stones in front of the fireplace for hours. I stared into the burning embers and one of the entities popped out from behind one, buzzed around, and came outside the grate to make sure I was okay. Then they all came out. I was the happiest little camper because they were all there, and I knew they always would be."

As Tony moved into his adolescence he discovered a passion for living in the fast lane and forgot about his spirit guides. Wild parties and wilder adventures were his forte, and he spent his young adulthood roaming the world, tasting the pleasures of exotic places. He was charming and articulate, gregarious and intelligent, and unabashedly hedonistic, qualities that made him a magnet for the kinds of trouble that create great stories later in life. For a few years he attended college but found it boring and staid; instead, he decided to become a hair designer, a profession in which he has enjoyed enormous success.

Tony's first professional job was at a trendy downtown salon that catered to an upscale clientele. One day a client started talking about astrology, a subject about which Tony knew nothing. Although he treasured his memories of "the little spirit friends" who had comforted him when he was young, he was not especially interested in spiritual subjects. Thus, he listened politely but noncommittally when his client raved about an astrologer whom he felt to be unusually gifted. Just before he finished cutting his client's hair, the client asked Tony where and when he had been born. Tony gave him that information reluctantly and then promptly forgot the conversation.

About six weeks later he was paged by the receptionist and told he had a personal call. "Well, that was unusual," Tony said. "No one ever called me at work. It turned out to be the astrologer to whom my client had given my birth information. She said I had an unusual astrological chart and she wanted to read it for me, free of charge. I didn't know her or what she was talking about but I thought it might be fun so I agreed to meet her at her house." Expecting to find an exotic gypsy swathed in stars and moons, Tony found instead an ordinary, suburban housewife who quietly sat him down and told him things that were impossible for her to know. "Specific things that had happened in my childhood," Tony exclaimed, "and physical things like the bad car accident that left me with scars because my legs had to be pinned back together. How could she know that? No one outside my immediate family knew that! The things she explained about me were so uncannily correct that I knew I should pay attention, but this was really a collision between my old world view and a new one." Besides telling him about himself, the astrologer urged him to take his life seriously because he was likely to die young. Although her insights intrigued him and made him somewhat more thoughtful about his life, he continued to live and play as much as before.

A few months later Tony was crossing a street when a ragged old man approached him and said that Tony needed to hear what he had to say. "Every hair on my body stood up," Tony recalled. "He was a homely guy, an old Indian, who said he lived nearby. I thought he was crazy and I went into a restaurant to get something to eat, but when I came out he was waiting for me. I didn't know what to think, but he was so insistent that I decided to go with him to his home. It turned out that he was a shaman. We sat in the dirt in his basement for about five hours and he told me things about my life, like where I was heading and what I needed to do to turn it around. He also warned me that I would die at the age of 33. When it was over, I remember walking outside and looking at the sky and thinking 'Thank you.' I was stunned, completely blown away by the experience. But, of course, I didn't heed his words and instead spent every day living life like ten people. Well, I didn't die at 33, but something else happened that left me a completely different person than I had been before."

What happened was the breakup of a cherished relationship, a loss that left Tony angry, confused, and inconsolably bereaved. His partner of many years abruptly walked out of his life, telling him he never wanted to see him again. "It was the single, most painful experience in my life," Tony said. "I was in a state of complete shock. I had everything I grew up believing a human being could possibly want: a business, a home, and a huge bank account. I traveled all over the world. There was nothing I wanted that I didn't have. And I had no inkling that anything was wrong. Everything had seemed so loving and harmonious. I always thought our relationship would last forever and I was devastated when it ended."

"Every night when I came home I kept my blinds closed. I lit a fire and sat in my rocking chair and read every self-help book I could find. I had stacks of them next to my chair. Then I read every spiritual book I could get my hands on by every spiritual teacher. I tried to talk on a recorder but that didn't work, so I started writing every day. Every single evening I'd look at my ceiling and say, 'what do you want me to know? What am I supposed to learn from this?' And several months later, the answer suddenly came that it was time for me to grow up spiritually, to start paying attention to the fact that I may be a physical and mental being but I also have a soul."

"That was really was the most incredible experience," Tony recalled. "Even talking about it now I have goosebumps. It was the most powerful moment in my life. Big Mama had to kick this determined Leo right where it hurt. She didn't take away my life, but she forced me to rearrange it. I realized about six months later that this was what the astrologer and the shaman had meant when they said I was going to die young. Old Tony *had* died and the person who emerged threw the blinds open on the spiritual part of me. I started to look carefully at everything that came along to see how it all fit together. I had to hit bottom to begin to have a mature faith that encompassed mind, body, and soul."

****

When I asked Dan, a former high school teacher and drama coach and now a psychologist and part-time college professor, about his spiritual experiences he first recalled something that had happened when he was 8-years-old. One morning Dan abruptly developed all the symptoms of what appeared to be acute appendicitis. Although his family members were devout practitioners of Christian Science, a religion that eschews conventional medical intervention in favor of faith healing, his mother decided to take him to a physician. The doctor who examined Dan determined that his appendix should be immediately removed.

"I went into a panic," Dan recalled, "because to be in a hospital, let alone have surgery, was unthinkable. And then I thought, 'I'm going to go full tilt and do everything I know, pray as hard as I can and access the spiritual force and really put it to the test and see if it works because I want it more than anything else.' There were about six hours between when I left the doctor's office and when I was supposed to check into the hospital. I went into my room and had this incredible sensation, lying on my bed, of feeling flooded with light. I guess that's the best way to put it. The sense came to me, it wasn't like a voice but a sense, that I was going to be just fine. Everything was going to be all right. At that moment I felt something washing through me and then the pain was gone. The experience only lasted for a few minutes but when it was done I *knew* that something had taken place, that there had been a miracle, that this was the possibility of spiritual healing that I had been hearing about all this time. And truly I became symptom free; there was no more pain from that point and it did not recur later. So I went back to the hospital and told the doctor I was fine now, and he said 'Hmm . . . must have been bloating or something else.' But I felt like I was on such a different level that I didn't care what he said. I thought, this really works, this is miracles and I can make them happen! That was the most significant experience of faith healing I ever had. Nothing that followed ever came close, maybe because I thought I knew how to make it happen and I didn't."

After this inexplicable experience of faith healing, Dan became an ardent Christian Scientist, attending church as often as he could until just before he graduated from high school. At the same time, however, his home life was deteriorating. He had grown up in his maternal grandparents' home because his father abandoned his mother before his birth. Dan's mother remarried when he was in middle school, but her new husband was addicted to alcohol, and shortly after the marriage, he became physically abusive to his new family. Initially, Dan took refuge in church and in food, growing obese by the time he was 12. But as the violence in his home escalated, he became disenchanted with his church's adamant denial of evil. The breaking point came on New Year's Eve when Dan was 17. "The stepfather had a bad alcoholic episode and was beating her and me, and I pulled a knife on him," Dan recalled. "Well, the police came and my mother decided she was going to leave him. She started the divorce process but changed her mind a few weeks later and went back to him. I remember giving up at that point, not so much on him as on her, and I, who had never touched a drop of alcohol, had not smoked, had very much lived this Christian Science straight and narrow life, started taking LSD in fairly massive quantities."

"And I loved it!" Dan exclaimed. "It was 1968 and I lived in San Francisco so I had plenty of access to great drugs and a great environment in which to take them. I also discovered that drugs were a good way to lose weight, and for awhile I even felt that doing hallucinogenic drugs really brought out my true self, which was being happy all the time. I never had any bad experiences. Of course, as kids on drugs at that time were bound to do, I figured out everything and had all these great insights, none of which I remember anymore," he laughed. "I also stopped going to church because it felt adulterous to belong to a church that prohibits the use of drugs when I was enjoying drugs. I didn't feel I could have it both ways."

Dan reveled in his newfound lifestyle for several years until one day he had a terrifying experience. "I had gone to visit some friends on Mt. Shasta," he recalled. "I took some speed to go for a stroll around the mountain. I went by myself, which was something I rarely did. I always liked being connected to people and I didn't want to be lonely. Suddenly I felt an overwhelming urge to kill myself. It came out of nowhere. I had never thought about suicide before, even during the bad times at home. Yet here I was having this powerful feeling while the sun was setting on the mountain. I remember wondering why I was thinking about suicide and realizing that the drug must have been inducing some kind of darkness. I was in a total panic and I reverted to my first defense, which was thinking about God. I decided to pray and I said to God, 'I tell You what. Get me through this unharmed and I won't do this anymore. It's just over, this period of taking drugs, because I think it's not all happy singing in Golden Gate Park.' And that was it. The suicidal feelings vanished as quickly as they had arrived, and I haven't done any recreational drugs since then because I've never wanted to tempt the fates."

This experience got Dan back on track, spiritually and vocationally. He began to feel a heightened sense of connection with the physical world and gained an awareness, reminiscent of Meister Eckhart, that "all that is is holy." Rather than return to his former church and religious beliefs, however, he became more universal in his orientation to the spiritual realm. "It's become more important to me to feel the energy that comes into me from other people and from the universe at large and the energy that flows out of me to them," Dan said. "It's made me feel that spirituality is a transaction, if you will, or an interaction with the life force, and that it's important to be able to open up and feel a part of the world around me and as much of the universe as I can."

****

"I don't talk about my spiritual experiences very much," Parwati confided when we began her interview for this book. Parwati is a popular university professor and the first woman from her country to be granted a Ph.D. by an American university. Her fierce intellect and passion for feminism exist side by side with her commitment to leading a spiritual life. When I asked her what kinds of spiritual experiences she had had, she looked away, drawn toward a private, inner space. "The first thing that comes to me is the time I asked my mother about my birth. It was when I was working on my dissertation and not finishing it as fast as I could. I didn't know why it was taking me so long so I meditated and I saw my hands flailing all about my head. It was weird, but I felt like it was very hard for me to get out of the womb. So I asked my mother whether her labor with me was especially difficult because of what I had seen in my meditation. At first she said no. Then she suddenly remembered that several weeks before my birth she went to see the midwife because I kept turning around in her womb. The midwife would straighten me out and send my mother home, but pretty soon I would be turning around again." Did this mean you were reluctant to be born? I wondered. Parwati smiled. "I thought I wanted to come as soon as I could. My mother and I laughed when she told me this, and she said, 'That's why you move around so much, because you want a challenge and to go somewhere else.'"

Parwati grew up in Indonesia, the fifth child in a close-knit family headed by devout Muslim parents. She was not aware of having any unusual spiritual abilities until she was afflicted by a mysterious illness when she was 12. Parwati remembers lying in bed and staring at the texture of the adjacent wall and then suddenly being able to see through it. As she watched the movement of the clouds she felt herself slip out of her body; then everything, even memory, disappeared. Several days later she regained consciousness and thereafter she could see things that were invisible to most other people, such as spiritual beings and energy fields around people's bodies. Parwati kept these perceptions to herself because her father considered them irrational and she was afraid he would not believe her. Her maternal grandmother was very spiritually attuned, however, and Parwati would listen with rapt attention to the stories she told about how her spiritual abilities helped her to raise nine children without a husband and to encourage her land to produce enough food for her large family. Although her grandmother told these stories to anyone who would listen, Parwati was the only one who took them to heart.

Her grandmother's advice proved providential years later when Parwati was struggling to end a 5-year relationship with a man who had become increasingly abusive. She had been trying to leave him for months, but because they were a well-known couple in their community and because her partner used mutual friends to dissuade her from leaving, Parwati could not manage to break free. One day when she was agonizing over what to do, her grandmother told her about a particular regimen of fasting and chanting that had helped her to accomplish emotionally difficult tasks. Parwati began to practice this regimen, and within a few days she felt a deep sense of release. "I don't know how to explain it," Parwati said. "It was like a switch was thrown and I came back to myself. I felt connected to the spiritual realm as I hadn't since I was a child, and that gave me the strength to leave my boyfriend. I knew I wasn't alone and that I could do this."

Shortly thereafter, Parwati decided to enter graduate school in the United States, returning to Indonesia a few years later to collect data for her doctoral dissertation. When she arrived home she discovered that a beloved sister was dangerously ill and unresponsive to conventional medical treatment. Parwati looked around for a traditional healer and was directed by a friend to a particular shaman. When she reached the shaman's home later that evening, she immediately perceived a multicolored band of energy around his head. After telling him what she saw, Parwati also confided some other spiritual experiences she had had, including an ability to touch people and occasionally heal them. The shaman listened attentively, told her what to do for her sister, and invited Parwati to study with him.

Her sister recovered fully, and Parwati spent the next two years as his apprentice. During this same time she was travelling periodically to remote villages throughout Indonesia to conduct her doctoral research and thus had numerous opportunities to practice what she was learning. "Wherever I went people would come to me with their problems," Parwati recalled. "These villagers were very poor and I found myself doing physical and spiritual healing simultaneously. That was important and very helpful for me personally as well as spiritually."

Although Parwati brought her healing skills with her when she returned to the United States, she has had to put them to different uses. "I don't practice shamanship here because I've found that most people aren't in tune with that kind of healing, or they're into evangelical healing which I'm not into at all," she said. "But I use these skills when I teach. They help me to be more attuned to my students and more tolerant of other points of view. They help me remember that teaching is an ancient profession that helps us learn from our mistakes in this and other lives. They help me see the spiritual light in everyone, even people who don't believe it's there. I stopped being a Muslim years ago, but there is something from that religion that I really love. When Allah created human beings, Allah blew a breath into each person. That means that we're not just dirty human beings who have to submit to Allah's will. There is something holy inside each of us because we're *part* of Allah. You know, the time we're living in right now is so awful. So much terrible stuff is going on that sometimes it's very hard to feel connected with the breath of Allah. I have to work on it. My healing abilities help me to remember that there is light and power outside and inside each of us, and that it really works."

****

Spiritual experiences like those recounted by my informants may be extraordinary, but they are only insights, and no insight, however powerful, magically produces psychological health or spiritual intelligence. Both demand active, sustained, and resolute effort. Yet, participants' spiritual experiences seemed to *crystallize* their commitment to psychological growth by introducing them to inner, spiritual depths of which they were previously unaware. Walters and Gardner (1986) used the concept of the *crystallizing experience* to describe the unusual and dramatic ways in which some individuals discover their talents and abilities. According to these researchers, crystallizing experiences trigger long-term changes in people's sense of self and profoundly affect the kind and quality of intellectual or creative work they eventually produce. Although their end point did not include spiritual intelligence, I believe the concept provides a powerful framework for understanding the potential impact of spiritual awareness on the human psyche.

CHAPTER FIVE

A New Frame of Mind

Clearly, one may reach the state of transcendence by many roads. . . . Once it is reached, we are no longer the same; we are compatriots with others who have crossed the chasm by various means.
—Molefi K. Asante (1984)

What does it mean to be psychologically healthy? This is a puzzle that has mystified students of human behavior for the past century, and it is far from solved. To some it means conforming to standards of thought and behavior espoused by the majority in any particular culture. To others, it means biochemical and neurological functionality. To most, it means being free of mental illness or symptoms of psychopathology (such as psychosis or antisocial behaviors). Psychological health comprises these elements, yet it is more than cultural or physiological normalcy. It includes the ability to operate rationally, with minimal emotional interference, while simultaneously feeling all one's emotions and acting on them appropriately. It includes the willingness to reflect, to be inner-directed, to take responsibility for one's life, and to learn from and adapt to changing circumstances. The ability to be autonomous and to articulate one's feelings and needs are critical components. Equally important are empathy and compassion, altruism, and the capacity to listen well to others. *Self-actualization* and *self-realization* are Western terms that suggest optimal states of well being in which one strives to live with integrity, to evolve a coherent sense of meaning and purpose, and to discover and express one's deepest values throughout one's life.

Does spiritual awareness have a role to play in the evolution of psychological health? Among many Western scientists and lay people, the answer would be "no." Unfortunately, that response is often perfunctory, arising more from prejudice and fear than from an open-minded exploration of the farther reaches of consciousness. Indeed, the nineteenth-century English poet and mystic, William Blake, lamented that "If the doors of perception were cleansed everything would appear to man as it is, infinite. For man has closed himself up, till he sees all things thro' narrow chinks in his cavern" (quoted in Underhill, 1911, p. 240).

But when a person enlarges these chinks and opens wider the doors of perception, deliberately or accidentally, positive changes can and do occur. A growing number of psychological studies have reported significant psychological growth in individuals who have had spiritual experiences compared with those who have not (e.g., Delmonte, 1980; Emmons, 1999; Greeley, 1974, 1987; Hay & Morisy, 1978; Hood, 1975; Noble, 1984; Nystul & Garde, 1977). In general, the former group demonstrates a higher level of well being on a wide variety of psychometric measures. People in this group appear to be significantly less authoritarian and prejudiced, more assertive, imaginative, self-sufficient, and relaxed (Mathes, Zevon, Roter, & Joerger, 1982). They are more inquiring, logical, and astute (Jewkes & Baruss, 2000), and show a more pronounced degree of emotional flexibility and self-control (Fite, 1981). They also evince a greater sense of meaning and purpose in life (Wuthnow, 1978). They are more compassionate and tolerant of individual differences, and more accepting of all parts of themselves—both the good and the bad (Noble, 1984, 1994). But *how* do these positive changes come about?

Unfortunately, psychologists have nothing comparable to Ultrasound and Positron Emission Tomography through which to monitor changes in the self. What we need is the ability to take time-lapse photographs of the evolving self because, like the coming of Spring, psychological growth happens gradually, often imperceptibly, until it reaches the point where change becomes apparent to oneself and to others. Without the psychological equivalent of the CT scan, we must rely on people's subjective reports about the unfolding of their inner lives and their relationships in—and to—the world.

In the last chapter, participants in my study described how their spiritual experiences encouraged them to look beyond the ideas that were limiting their psychological realities and their daily lives. Their experiences offered them a glimpse of the multidimensional nature of the self and encouraged them to live more consciously with that awareness. However powerful these experiences were, they are only insights and no insight automatically results in greater well being. Yet if a person is ready and willing, spiritual experiences can promote a resurgence of psychological growth. According to my informants, their growth occurred most noticeably in five particular areas. These were: (a) a greater understanding of and ability to endure adversity; (b) a conscious rejection of self-destructive attitudes and behaviors; (c) a newfound or renewed ability to recognize and utilize inner resources; (d) an enhanced acuity of feeling, especially compassion and empathy, for oneself and for others; and (e) a commitment to participate more fully in what Underhill called "the joyous travail of the universe" (1911, p. 447). These areas of growth will be explored more fully next.

One of the first changes that most participants noticed was a deeper understanding—and acceptance—of the role of adversity in their lives. Although psychological growth is an integral part of human development, it is a process that many people ignore until illness and loss, disappointment or trauma, brings it to the fore. Adverse experiences are ubiquitous in human life, no matter how one tries to insulate oneself from them. How one responds to adversity is a determining factor in psychological health, but that response demands more than good coping skills and effective defense mechanisms. Without an acceptance of the necessity—and inevitability—of challenge and change, one can find oneself in serious psychological trouble.

Adversity threatens one's view of oneself and one's place in the world. The more severe or relentless its nature, and the earlier it occurs in a person's life, the more deleterious its effects can be. Adversity can wear down the most resilient individual, leaving one feeling psychologically numb or alienated from life. It can rupture relationships and make one act out one's rage and pain on others, particularly those who are vulnerable and powerless. It can lead to self-destruction through drug or alcohol addiction and other forms of reckless behavior, and it often results in suicide. Several of my informants were trapped in destructive emotional states prior to their spiritual awakenings. Their experiences helped them realize that misfortune has meaning that goes far beyond primitive notions of punishment and reward, victimization by capricious gods, or random acts of a senseless universe.

For example, Maya's insight during her Thanksgiving wake-up call that she was *for life* as opposed to death made her realize that she had to learn how to live. "I was in big trouble," she said. "I needed help. I was dying. I had been in therapy for years, but for the first time I realized that I needed to learn how to *live*. After my experience I was able to tell my sister that I was truly committed to life and would never try to kill myself again, even if I wanted to. I thought that would be the end of it, but what I didn't realize was that it was going to take me years to unlearn dying and learn how to live. Prior to my attempt I had put myself in tons of dangerous situations. Everybody thought I was so brave, but actually I was suicidal. It wasn't until two years after this insight that I actually became afraid of death! For me that was an amazing turnaround."

As Maya reflected on her journey since that memorable Thanksgiving, she acknowledged that she wasn't yet fully recovered. Yet her spiritual awakening helped her accept that becoming—and staying—well would be an ongoing process. "I still struggle with being self-destructive," Maya said. "But I've discovered that I can talk from the position of someone who has wrestled with these issues and help other people who are trying to heal. It was a big shift for me to move from feeling totally victimized and incapable of coping, to coping and being able to help other people cope. And it happened because I had a supreme moment of non-coping! But now I am able to say to them and to myself, 'Yeah, life can be devastating and I'm sorry. If I could spare you I would, but you need to feel terrible right now and I can't take that away from you because there's something around the corner. You won't ever see it unless you get there, and you will.'"

It is "a shocking thing to know so much about oneself in such a little time" (Lester, 1983, p. 31). It is this moment of profound awareness than can crystallize the desire and motivation to be well, for it is precisely tailored to the immediate psychological needs of each individual. Maya's experience enabled her to staunch the flood of pain and rage that had turned her against her own being. Tomas' experience helped him to move beyond the myopia of constricting psychological habits.

When Tomas encountered what he called the "threshold," he felt, for the first time, a self-acceptance that would have profound repercussions in his life. "I had always felt insecure about being socially acceptable and keeping up in some material way with the rest of the world," Tomas said, "but my threshold experience gave me a new place to stand on. I've become much less frantic and desperate than I was for most of my life. I would say that a kind of restless, unhappy, low-level panic and insecurity were my basic emotions during most of my life. I always felt like a tremendous personal failure. I'm quite capable of still feeling that; I can't say that it's gone. But there are certainly times when I feel calm, when I can look at myself and think I turned out pretty well. And that's a very powerful kind of change."

This discovery enabled Tomas to begin opening up parts of himself that had been tightly shut for years. "I'm a person who used to think that people who didn't dress in 'straight' clothes were weird, that people who played drums were dangerous, that people who didn't live in normal, clean houses and take showers every day were derelicts. I was a very intolerant, judgmental, and narrow person, but I've become much more open. I find that I have compassion for other people. That wasn't the kind of family that I came from and it certainly was not true of my childhood. And not only am I capable of compassion, but it's so tremendously enriching for me. I've discovered that I've become very nonjudgmental about other people although I can still be judgmental if I'm feeling insecure. To find a really strong vein in myself of tremendous acceptance for people for what they are has been astounding. For instance, I have a deep admiration and affection for gay men, for lesbians, for bisexuals, although I certainly can't look back into my own past and see where that comes from. That may be the strongest or clearest example of what I'm talking about, but it isn't the only one. I've also started to cultivate some of my feminine qualities. Sometimes I don't feel like a 'real' man because I'm interested in developing parts of me that 'real men' aren't supposed to care about, but I no longer care. In fact I prefer not to be that kind of man."

For every person who participated in this study, a spiritual awakening was a powerful and necessary reminder that what we call the "unconscious" is, in fact, vibrant and deeply conscious. Further, each realized that it was his or her responsibility as a human being to grow in psychological breadth and depth. These realizations mark the beginning of spiritual intelligence. When one accepts responsibility for the totality of one's life, psychological growth ceases to be happenstance and becomes intentional. One makes the choice to live deliberately and to learn how best to live one's life. One begins to pay close attention to internal cues as well as external experiences and to allow spiritual resources to help one navigate difficult emotional waters.

Prior to my spiritual awakening I had fallen into a deep depression, one that was precipitated by the continuing estrangement from my parents. Although I was not suicidal I thought often about death. My mother had rejected me from birth and said that she wished I had never been born. As I grew older and her family grew larger, her abusive and capricious behavior escalated. I lived in constant fear for my sanity and that of my siblings. Years later, a former neighbor would confide that my mother was the coldest person she had ever known, but neither she nor anyone else intervened on our behalf. I had always felt a deep determination to preserve my own soul, and so I actively resisted my mother's destructive influence until I was old enough to leave home. But the price I had to pay—permanent exile from my family of origin—was higher than I realized it would or could be. The full impact of that awareness hit me with gale force when I was 25, along with the realization that desperation rather than deliberation had been driving all of my major life decisions.

It is difficult to convey how essential my spiritual awakening was to my physical survival and psychological recovery. Certainly, it comforted me enormously by answering my most urgent questions about the meaning, purpose, and continuity of being. Yet, far more enlivening was a breathtaking sense of being known fully and fully loved regardless of the strengths, weaknesses, gifts, and flaws that I brought to this physical existence. This awareness stabilized my sense of self, placed my pain in a larger context, and helped free me from the despair that was careening out of control. It set me on an active journey of healing, and it led me to leave law for psychology, a field in which I had no prior interest. It taught me that the inner senses were powerful allies that could be called on to help solve problems and to find new life directions, and it became a cornerstone of the work I do with my students and clients. It also led to an unusual resolution of my estrangement from my parents.

Several years ago I had the following dream. I was seated at a table in an attorney's office facing my father while my mother looked on from a distance. We were there to settle my lawsuit for emotional damages sustained over a lifetime of calculated rejection. Although I had anticipated a protracted legal battle, my father suddenly capitulated, admitted culpability, and offered to settle despite his fear that the damages would be ruinous. As my attorney began to negotiate the settlement I looked at my father, who seemed old, resigned, and very tired, and then at my mother, who was charred by a rage that had burned out of control. Suddenly I was flooded with compassion and sorrow. I reached out a hand to restrain my attorney and said to my parents, "I release you from your debt, and I release myself from having to collect it." Then I turned, walked out of the office, and awoke, feeling psychologically free in a way I had never been before. That freedom continues to this day, as does our physical estrangement.

Valerie had a dream that was similarly transforming. After she returned home from her flight to California, she began a difficult, sometimes torturous journey of psychological healing. She has spent many years regaining her sense of direction and learning to focus her energies, stay sober, and choose the right people and situations in her life. There have been many times when she wanted to quit, many times when the pain and effort of healing were more than she could bear. She remembered one night when she was having a horrible argument with her boyfriend on the phone and feeling both rage and despair. Suddenly an electrical outage occurred.

"The phone went dead, and there was nothing I could do," Valerie recalled. "I felt very unsafe, like a vulnerable child hiding in the corner, crying and afraid. I couldn't watch television or read so I decided to sit quietly and try to muster up the adult part of me to nurture that inner child. Then I had a kind of waking dream in which I went down into a cave that I realized was the darker side of my consciousness."

"Immediately before me was a figure wearing my black hat and kimono. I had the sense that I had come to a place I had never been before without alcohol. The figure looked around at me and I saw that it *was* me and that shocked and frightened me. I saw a glimpse of bitterness and also an incredible intelligence that had deflected a lot of my pain. When I looked around I saw broken parts of my body all over the cave. I think that this figure possessed me when I was drinking. Now it no longer possessed me, but I was seeing it clearly for the first time. And it was looking at me as if to say, *There is a lot more I can do besides stay down here and hide this mess.* It was amazing. I know I was far from the small child in the corner at that point, that my psyche was being transformed by an incredible creative surge. I felt that I had tapped into a very fertile part of my being. I was both seeing this figure and being the figure that I saw. It was a very ancient, archetypal figure; there was much more to it than just 'me.' As the dream ended I saw myself coming out of the cave, taking off the black hat and the kimono, lying on a beach with my toes in the water, and feeling that the ocean was my family, my friend, and myself. I went from seeing different aspects of myself to letting myself feel at one with a new self-knowledge."

This dream deeply altered Valerie's sense of who she was. It made her realize that her inner self was not just an abstract concept and that she could rely on that self for help. Valerie seemed to glow as she recalled the profound connection she had experienced with her larger self and said she knew that if she sat quietly, in what she called contemplation, she could contact it at any time. "I like distractions and so sometimes I'll stay away a little longer than I should," Valerie laughed. "But eventually I'll take a breath, become quiet, and try to hear what it wants to tell me. And it never fails to tell me what I need to hear."

Why do spiritual awakenings counteract the despair and myopia that often precede them? Because they are vivid reminders that we are spiritual beings on a physical journey, one that allows us to experience an enormous range of thoughts, emotions, and corresponding events. When these complex phenomena are seen in their spiritual or *metapsychological* context, a person's trust can be restored "in the continuity of life, the order of nature, and the transcendent order of the divine" (Herman, 1992, p. 51). In order to take the risk to grow psychologically, to be creative, compassionate, and aware, this sense of trust must be firmly rooted in an individual's psyche. When it is compromised or destroyed, a person becomes extremely vulnerable to psychological disorders ranging from depression to sociopathy. As Jung discovered in his own life, a spiritual awakening reminds us that "life is a segment of existence which is enacted in a three-dimensional boxlike universe especially set up for it" (1965, p. 295). It shows us that life is deliberately chosen, rather than randomly assigned, and that our physical existence is a small part of a larger reality in which we are firmly embedded. This knowledge is inherent in all of us but it is easily overwhelmed by the vicissitudes of daily life. Thus, a spiritual awakening can bring it back into sharp focus.

Tony could have become embittered and apathetic when he lost his beloved partner and plunged into the bottomless grief that results from rejection. Instead, he reached into the depths of his soul and was rewarded with a spiritual awakening that proved a turning point in his life. Tony's awakening did not strip him of his zest for life, but it made him realize that there was more to life than the pursuit of pleasure. It taught him that neither a relationship nor affluence could satisfy his deepest needs and that a severe emotional shock was the best means by which his inner self could finally command his attention. As a result of his awakening, Tony reorganized his priorities and began to work daily on his psychological growth, not just in moments of crisis.

Tony is not religious, nor does he pray or meditate in conventional ways, but he has evolved his own way of staying connected to his inner self. "I talk, think, and communicate freely with the world around me, with friends, my clients, the trees, and the spiders on my porch. I work on being kinder to the world and how I participate in it. I had given lip service to paying attention before this experience, but now I really have to do it. I have a strong personality and sometimes I can be very self-centered and overpowering. I work daily on keeping clear with myself and letting other people be as important to me as I am to myself. This experience was a wake-up call to move to a deeper level of understanding, to integrate my male and female selves, to be grateful for participating in life. I don't take that for granted anymore. Every day I work on being just a good old human being whose mind, body, and soul are all together because then other people will pay attention too."

Several years ago Tony tested positive for HIV, an event that showed him how much he had grown. "When I got the test results the HIV management team asked if they could help me with any psychological stuff. I said no, not because I was in denial, but because I really felt OK with the news. I know we're all going to die and I'm looking forward to what comes next, but I'll continue to live as fully as I can until that happens. Amazingly enough, my T-cell count continues to go up and astounds my doctor. I feel complete because I realize that I've done everything I set out to do, but I know that I can still positively affect the world around me until the day I die."

Susan's encounter with the medicine Buddha was a turning point in her life as well. In the weeks following this experience she realized that she needed to heal more than just her physical body. Although tracking down the cause of her mysterious neurological symptoms was a formidable task, she also had to face daunting psychological challenges. She had to accept the fact that her family had never been and would never be there for her no matter how hard she tried to be the perfect daughter. She had to come to terms with the sexual and physical abuse meted out by her father, her mother's vindictive jealousy, and their absolute denial of responsibility for any wrongdoing. Susan had to see how her childhood pain was leaching into her adulthood and poisoning her adult relationships. Finally, she had to decide to live fully in the face of what appeared to be an irreversible and degenerative disability.

Over the next several years Susan tenaciously pursued various physical and psychological therapies, staying with each until she had learned all that she could. She tried different forms of meditation, studied nutrition and biophysical energy fields, and even met once with the Dalai Lama's personal physician. She read copiously about sexual abuse and multiple sclerosis and talked to anyone she thought might provide some answers or a fresh perspective on healing. Although all these activities proved helpful to varying degrees, Susan is convinced that her spiritual awakening was the critical link in the chain of events that helped her to pull her life together. "My experience with the Medicine Buddha is what put me consciously on a spiritual path and forced me to seek answers in places I had never looked before," Susan confided. "With that I knew that there was another realm. I knew that we are eternal beings and all connected. There was no longer faith, belief, anything like that. I truly believe that experience made me begin to figure out who I am."

Gradually Susan began to notice changes in herself. First there was a shift from what she called *human doing* to *human being*. "My way of coping with the craziness of my family was to do," she explained. "Be a student, do well in school, make things, cook. But I couldn't do anything when I became ill. I had to learn how to be, which was very, very hard. Before I always had ways to distract my attention from the pain; now I had to be with it. That was tough." As Susan learned to sit with pain she became calmer and more insightful, and she started to look at her suffering in a different way. No longer did it seem like random misfortune but rather a deliberate impetus to growth. "I always wondered why I've gone through so much pain in my life, but I began to realize that on some level I wanted and needed to learn something. That's a tough one to swallow because why would anyone set herself up for incest, physical abuse, illness, and abandonment? But that explanation makes sense to me. I find I need a lot more time by myself now just to stay centered. I feel much better when I meditate a little every day. I don't always do that but when I don't I find myself doing things that don't feel quite right. So that's a big part of this change too, learning to be more in harmony with my inner self and watching what I'm doing on a daily basis."

"It's also made me more aware in my daily interactions with other people," Susan continued. "I'm not always charming and cheerful, but I enjoy having the opportunity to touch another life. I enjoy realizing that we're all on separate spiritual paths whatever our level of awareness. I'm not interested in how much money I can make or how much someone else has and that has made me less willing to spend my time around people who are living in a very superficial way. Now I want to spend time with people who are deeply aesthetically or spiritually connected. And it's made me look at other people's suffering with more compassion and detachment. For example, I get less tolerant of people being horrible to each other, but at the same time I realize that violence is just another experience here on Earth. I may abhor it and I don't want to be involved in it, but there's something to be learned from that too."

About three years after her spiritual awakening, Susan had a dream that helped her solve the mystery of her physical illness. "In my dream I was working with chemicals in a laboratory and not very happy," Susan said. "I started praying, which is not something I do when I'm awake, and I realized that I could rise out of my body, float upwards, and regulate my height with the intensity of the prayer. At one point I looked down on the lab and saw my body, and then I was moving into the clouds. The further I went the more aware I became of a very intense light. It would have been blinding if I hadn't been asleep. It wasn't painful, just extremely intense and ecstatic. Then I realized that I was seeing Christ. He was standing in the classic pose with his hands out forward, radiating this unconditional love into the universe. There wasn't a concrete person there; it was more the suggestion of a body. As I stood to the side of him and was washed with this incredible energy, I realized that through my prayer I could stay close to him. But I also realized that the love he was radiating had nothing to do with me. It was completely impersonal; the love was for everyone. I had no sense that he even acknowledged my presence and, although that was a little disappointing, it really wasn't important. I stayed by his side for awhile and then I slowly went back down into my body and woke up."

"That was the most intense experience of ecstasy that I have ever had," Susan recalled. "I think the experience was more than a dream because the feelings stayed with me for quite awhile. It was strange because I'm not a Christian. I remember wondering why Christ appeared when I thought it should have been Buddha. I now think that the Christ energy is the one I associate with that feeling of ecstatic love because of my upbringing." I asked Susan what the purpose of this dream had been. "Well, when it happened I was feeling a lot of confusion about what I was going to do with my life because I was so ill," she replied. "I didn't find out about the misdiagnosis of multiple sclerosis until several years later, so a very important part of the dream's message was that I would be healed. It gave me the confidence that I didn't have to keep looking for answers. I didn't know that I was going to be physically healed, but I knew that things would be okay. And sure enough, a few years later I was working with chemicals in a lab when I learned that I had been misdiagnosed, and it was through my work there that I was able to get health insurance and get things sorted out."

Different spiritual awakenings serve different psychological needs. Tony's and Maya's taught them how to cope with adversity rather than be destroyed by it; Valerie's taught her to turn inward for answers to emotional and personal problems. I learned an acceptance of life and a capacity for forgiveness that I had been incapable of before, and Susan discovered the means to her psychological and physical restoration. Although spiritual experiences are unique to each person, they share a common purpose: to shock our waking selves out of their complacency and, as Tomas found, "to set us back on track."

When Megan's son was killed in an automobile accident, she was devastated. To cope with her grief she sought counseling and spiritual guidance, she participated in support groups, and she talked with her family and friends. Although these actions helped to some extent, something was missing. Megan felt she needed a creative outlet through which to express her feelings about her son's death and her near-death experience, but she had never thought of herself as an artist, nor was she aware that she had any artistic abilities. One day she found a boulder on her property and decided to make it a memorial to her son. She moved the boulder closer to the family home and then asked a local stonemason to teach her his craft. He said he could show her how to use the tools of his trade, but he could not tell her how or what to carve. "I remember him telling me it had to come from within," Megan said. "I don't think there's anything that anyone has ever said to me that's been more significant in terms of what I needed to hear. I didn't know what that meant so I sat by the stone trying to listen to myself. Nothing happened. Then one day I went out and started hammering away on it. Gradually a little creature started coming out. I could see its face but not its body and the more I tried, the more frustrated I got. At one point I stopped thinking and just hammered and chiseled in a fury.

When I stopped I saw a pattern of little heart-shaped leaves where the body was supposed to be. It's hard to describe what I felt then. It was such a powerful moment. I had an enormous sense that my intuition was real and that I could approach a stone with a feeling of trust instead of deliberateness. I knew then that something would always come."

In the years since her son's death, Megan has become an accomplished stone sculptor whose work has brought comfort to many people. She carves unique symbols on her stones, messages that speak to particular individuals. "I don't always know what the message is when I start to carve," Megan said, "but something always comes through. When I'm showing my work I always wonder how much I can say about this because I know that the process goes right to the very core of who and what I am; it's my connection with the life force. People always ask me what my symbols mean but not everybody really wants to know. Just the other day an elderly lady was looking at a stone and she asked me that question and I said, 'They will speak to you and tell you what they mean. They mean something to me but if they are to mean anything at all to you, they'll speak to you.' And this little old lady told me that when she was in Campfire Girls, her nickname had been 'Lightning' because she loved to move so fast. I had carved a lightning bolt going through a sun on the stone she was looking at, so I told her it was for her. That's the way it is. The stones speak in their own way to people and they say whatever the person needs to hear as long as he or she is open to it. Sometimes people are just bowled over by it, and sometimes they just see pretty little designs. I found that I don't have to say very much at all. I guess it has to do with allowing my inner self to say what it wants through the stone. It has its own voice."

"You know," Megan said quietly, "my son's body is gone but I still feel quite close to his spirit. In fact, his spirit is what's driving my stonework. His death and my stonework have taught me that there truly is a greater power. I feel connected to it, and that gives me a better sense of place and reason and of responsibility for being here. There is no longer faith, belief, anything like that. I *know* there's another realm. I *know* that we are eternal beings, that we are all connected in that plane. That knowing has affected my life profoundly. I was told that I would feel anger and bitterness and a whole range of emotions after the accident, but I have a hard time feeling really angry toward that truck driver. I have very legitimate reasons for feeling bitter because he made very bad choices. He knew he had bad brakes and should not have been on that road. But my experience made a real difference. Certainly I've felt rage and despair; when you've lost a child all those emotions are present, and yet his death has also been a gift. It was as if someone handed me my papers and said, 'This is your life.' I wasn't about to turn that down although I had no idea what it meant to take that responsibility on. I'm getting a better sense of what it means as I evolve."

A spiritual shock may be the catalyst that jumpstarts most people's psychological growth, but it does not lead to spiritual intelligence without a decision to participate more fully in the "joyous travail of the universe." This does not mean that an individual is called on to save the world, but to recognize that each of us is an integral part of a larger whole in which we are intimately and inextricably connected. "It takes a moist heart to walk with our brothers and sisters," a Native American tradition holds, "a moist heart to be at peace with ourselves, a moist heart to serve people well" (Fox, 1981, p. 329). Spiritual awakenings are meant to moisten our hearts and to be *active leavens for life* (King, 1980). They are neither justifications nor excuses for narcissism, grandiosity, fanaticism, or cruelty, nor are they avenues for psychological withdrawal. They are meant to remind us of the vast, rich universe within our own selves, amplify our capacity for intimacy and empathy, and to strengthen our willingness to relate well to others. They also show us that each person's psychological and spiritual health are inescapably tied to the health of the larger community.

Dan currently supervises counselors-in-training at a private university and maintains an extensive psychotherapy practice. He believes that his spiritual experiences are central to his work as a psychologist and to the depth of feeling he is able to offer other people. "They've made me more receptive to other people's feelings, more available, more empathic, less quick to judge. They've also helped me to integrate the things that happened to me in my childhood and adolescence. My psychological health is a direct product of my spiritual development. I don't see how else I would be functional to the extent that I have been because it provides me with a sense of confidence in myself and in the good will of others, and a willingness to be vulnerable. I think in some ways that's what psychotherapy is founded on, an ability to interact with people in a way that is transformative, whether that's the experience of being understood, or feeling supported or comforted in some way. The work I do is really difficult. Probably a third of my patients are terminally ill or will be at some point. I help people cope with pain and tragedy, with illness and death, and I couldn't do it without a foot in the spiritual world. I have to be conscious, aware, and spiritually present no matter what challenges my patients or I encounter."

For Valerie, spirituality is intimately related to citizenship and responsibility. "As you honor your own process of unfolding, you're able to honor others," she said. "It helps me be more self-aware so that I can be responsive but not reactionary, and empathic but not overwhelmed. It helps me to not run from the truth and to share my experiences without projecting them onto someone else. It gives me a sense of community and helps me to be strong enough to ask for help when I need it and caring enough to see problems that need to be addressed. It helps me see the beauty underneath because I realize that no matter how bad it gets, there's still something that's bigger."

Tomas shared a similar observation. "Whatever it is that is my spirit or is spiritual reality seems to me to be tremendously important and much more real than most of what we occupy ourselves with most of the time. Maybe that's because I came from a family that denied it so absolutely. It's hard for me to separate my political self from my feelings about spirituality. I feel a tremendous contempt for most of the values that this society holds. I think there's something fundamentally cruel and anti-spiritual about Western civilization. I look at things like the extermination of indigenous peoples and the mean-spirited brutality of Reagan-Bush politics, for example, and they seem to me to be the heart, the essence, and the bedrock of Western civilization. I feel that the material level of luxury that we think is necessary and desirable for life on this planet is inextricably linked with enormous suffering because we can only live this way at the expense of huge numbers of people and force that at gunpoint. When I think about the links between spirituality and the health of the psyche I get excited because I see those going seamlessly together."

Prior to his spiritual awakening, Tomas felt that his life was a conveyor belt to mediocrity with no way off. "I was being carried into the most horrifyingly normal, white, middle-class existence and there was nothing I could do about it," he said. "But after my threshold experience I started to feel that I *could* do something about it and that's been wonderful." Tomas became more attentive to social issues and then decided to act. He quit his full-time job and became a freelance technical writer so that he would have time for political activities. He began to participate in men's groups that grappled with and sought to redefine masculinity, and he became active in a feminist organization that works to prevent violence toward women. He also made a decision to live as lightly on the Earth as possible. "All the things that I used to center my life around, like material things and making money, now seem like things you do like breathing because on some level they need to be done. I know now that's not what life's about. That's been an enormous change."

In the early stages of this project, my psychiatrist friend asked me what difference it made whether people were spiritually aware as long as they functioned well in their lives. The best answers to that question come from my informants. Maya is convinced that she would neither be alive nor psychologically sound were it not for the Thanksgiving wake-up call she received, and her subsequent realization that the universe would bring her what she needed if she could get out of its way. "I've had so many of these experiences since then that you'd think I'd quit being surprised by now," she exclaimed. "But every time I'm struck anew with the wonder of it all." Megan is certain that if she did not feel a core of spirituality in herself, there would be no point in remaining alive. "What's the point if I'm of sound body and mind but I haven't got a heart, a soul, wherever that spirituality lies?" she asked.

Spirituality holds a similarly central place in Susan's life. "My experience with the Medicine Buddha is what put me consciously on a spiritual path and forced me to seek answers in places I had never looked before. With that experience I knew that there was another realm. I knew that we are eternal beings and all connected. There was no longer faith, belief, anything like that. I truly believe that experience made me begin to figure out who I am. I am definitely saner in the sense of being clearer about who I am, more grounded and centered. There's a certainty, a knowingness that I equate with sanity. When I start feeling out of touch with myself I get reminded and brought back. I pay attention to that now. I've learned that when I'm on the right track the pieces seem to fall in place and that I can ask for guidance. For a long time I felt I was lost in the woods and didn't know where to turn or what to do. Now I feel there are reasons for everything even if I may not know what they are, and that comforts me. I also take comfort from knowing that we are eternal beings. As a doctor, a lot of people ask me what happens when we die, and I tell them I don't know but I have no doubt that we continue. I realize that not many people share that sense; they take it on faith, but mine is a very different experience."

Tony feels it would be impossible to live his life fully "without aligning the body, the mind, and the soul as well as I possibly can. I won't even say 'think;' I know it's not possible. My spiritual self needs to be powerful and paid attention to." Alex concurs. "When I was trying to think my way through my depression, what I was looking for was underneath it all the time . . . a peace, a beauty already there. It's great to know that the Universe is really responsive to the needs of all us little preschoolers over here and that it's unpredictable in the ways that it responds and expresses itself. I have a real sense that there's a real kind of protectiveness. That's what I really want to say. I feel really protected in a certain way."

Dan looked surprised when he considered this question. "If you had asked me at the beginning of this interview how spirituality affects my life or my psychological health, I would have said 'I don't talk about spirituality much, I don't think about it much, I don't really go to church.' But listening to myself talk about my life, particularly in terms of my spiritual development, I realize it pretty much *is* my life. And my work and my sense of self are based upon it. I didn't know that."

Tomas fell silent as he thought about what he wanted to say. When he spoke, his words reminded me of something that Sobrahani Basu, an Indian scholar, wrote: "The highest value for all true mystics, whether Hindu, Buddhist, Jain, Christian, or Jew, is compassion—and the highest goal is to enable all the souls in existence to develop sufficient strength to be in conscious touch with the Divine Reality" (1983, p. 391). "I had a dream recently," Tomas said. "I had been reading a poem by Rumi which said, 'I who have come from the eternal silence and seem to be on my way thither . . . ', and that night I dreamt that I was at work watching a colleague give a presentation to a customer. Now, this colleague happens to be a very nondescript, very pudgy and pedestrian guy, someone to whom I haven't felt at all connected. But as soon as he finished his presentation, he started to do the ritual farewell dance of the temple goddess. There was a moment when he looked me in the eyes and seemed to say, 'Oh, I know what I am, I'm nondescript, I'm flat-footed, I lack grace, and here I am doing this incredible dance.' As I watched him, everything fell away until the only things left were his eyes and his hands. And then suddenly I saw the stars behind him and realized that the whole universe was the backdrop of life. I was no longer seeing him, I was seeing the spirit who brings us here and the spirit who takes us away. And this spirit said, 'I brought you here out of nothingness and when you're through I'll take you back. This time is so beautiful. Use it well.'"

"Every person . . . who awakens to consciousness of a Reality which transcends the normal world of sense—however small, weak, imperfect that consciousness may be—is put upon a road which follows at low levels the path which the mystic treads at high levels" (Underhill, 1911, p. 445). This is the road to spiritual intelligence, a frame of mind that offers the possibility of extraordinary awareness and extraordinary growth. But like any talent or skill, it is unattainable without extraordinary effort. We must *want* to cultivate this frame of mind, *want* to evolve our spiritual awareness, and *want* to integrate it into our lives in psychologically healthy and productive ways. For as the Kabalistic masters steadfastly maintained, "It is no great feat to 'enter the garden of heavenly visions'. . . . The trick is getting out again with our life and sanity intact" (Hoffman, 1981, p. 214).

CHAPTER SIX

Spiritual Intelligence or Spiritual Dementia

It is the most difficult of journeys but it has the greatest of rewards—self-discovery and self-mastery.
—Phil Nuernberger (1994)

Spiritual teachers have always advised their students to exercise caution where spiritual experiences are concerned. For example, a medieval tale about four Jewish sages who found their way to Paradise was used by generations of rabbis to forewarn their followers about the dangers inherent in these experiences. The first sage became so enamored of spiritual reality that he could not bear to return to physical life, and didn't. The second was psychologically overwhelmed by the experience and lost his mind. The third could not reconcile his experience with his religious training and left his faith to seek answers elsewhere. Only the fourth "ascended and descended in peace" (Hoffman, 1981). According to Howard Schwartz (1993), a scholar of Jewish mystical folklore, a person was considered "sufficiently grounded to be trusted with these dangerous subjects" only if he was male, at least 40 years of age, married with children, and learned in the Talmud (p. 30).

Others teachers have placed different restrictions on candidates who aspired to spiritual awareness. The mystery schools of the ancient Eastern world chose only an elite group of priests and scholars to develop higher consciousness. Buddhist and Christian monasteries offered training to celibate women and men who pursued spiritual growth within the confines of the cloister and a strict regimen of fasting and prayer. Carlos Castaneda (1985, 1991) was a contemporary anthropologist who, like Parwati, apprenticed himself to a shaman and underwent rigorous psychological preparation prior to exploring the spiritual realm.

Why do reputable spiritual teachers urge so much caution? Earlier I suggested that some people reject the idea or reality of spiritual phenomena either because they fear religious persecution or because they believe—or want to believe—that these experiences have purely physical explanations. But the caution that spiritual masters advise stems from another source—the potential of these experiences to change us for better or for worse depending on what we do with them. In this chapter I explore what I consider to be the most serious challenges inherent in these experiences, and the importance of psychological balance, motivation, humility, and integrity to the development of spiritual intelligence.

The awareness that physical reality is only one dimension of a larger reality in which we have our roots can enrich a person's life enormously, but it is not always easy to live with. In his pioneering study of religious experiences, William James (1902) noted that

> Religious mysticism is only one half of mysticism. The other half has no accumulated traditions except those which the text-books on insanity supply. Open any one of these, and you will find abundant cases in which "mystical ideas" are cited as characteristic symptoms of enfeebled or deluded states of mind. In delusional insanity, paranoia . . . we may have a *diabolical* mysticism, a sort of religious mysticism turned upside down. (1902, p. 417; emphasis in original)

James was referring to the fact that spiritual experiences can resemble and occasionally induce what Western psychologists refer to as *psychosis*, a serious mental illness in which a person's thought processes and ability to function in physical reality are seriously impaired. That was the fate of the medieval rabbi who lost his mind. The most common symptoms of psychosis are visual and auditory hallucinations and cognitive distortions, some of which can be religious or spiritual in nature. With rare exceptions (e.g., Lukoff & Everest, 1985; Wapnick, 1972) psychotic episodes are not known to improve an individual's life, but as my informants found, spiritual experiences can crystallize a person's desire for psychological health and commitment to live in harmony with the world. What, then, can turn these experiences "upside down"?

One critical factor is motivation. When the quest for spiritual awareness becomes a substitute for satisfying work or interpersonal relationships—or when it fosters an unhealthy dependency on another person, group, or spiritual practice—it places a person at grave psychological risk. This is the trap that a large number of people fell into when they surrendered their autonomy to the Reverend Jim Jones and later were expected-or forced-to participate in a mass suicide at Jonestown. It is a trap that can ensnare anyone who abdicates responsibility for his or her life. A former client, whom I shall call Sarah, was able to extricate herself from such a trap, but not before she was almost irreparably wounded.

Sarah had grown up in a family that was riddled with psychopathology and she desperately wanted to avoid a similar fate. She had always been intuitive and interested in psychic phenomena, so she searched for an esoteric explanation that would help her make sense of her painful life experiences and give them meaning. Her search led her to explore a variety of spiritual movements, and eventually she put herself in the hands of a spiritual advisor who taught her to hypnotize herself to achieve inner peace. This advisor also encouraged Sarah to use various methods of divination, such as randomly selected passages from books, to make decisions and solve problems. Unfortunately, the advisor did not encourage her to deal with the underlying issues that were causing her psychological distress, nor to do the difficult, sometimes tedious, but necessary work of healing. By divorcing her search for solace from her intellectual understanding, and by refusing to unravel the complex strands of pain that imprisoned her, Sarah made little progress toward her goal of psychological growth. Instead she became more passive and withdrawn and increasingly dependent on her advisor for emotional support. One day, during a self-hypnosis session, Sarah entered into a terrifying altered state of consciousness. She felt as though she had been sucked out of her body and into a nightmarish vortex that was overflowing with a lifetime's accumulated anger and grief. When she finally managed to extricate herself from this vortex and return to her body she was physically ill, and for many days her thoughts and feelings were extremely disjointed. Sobered and scared by this experience, Sarah turned to her advisor for help, but her advisor attributed it to an encounter with evil and told Sarah to pray rather than try to understand it. Fortunately, Sarah was frightened enough to look further afield for assistance, and several weeks later she entered psychotherapy with me.

For many people, spiritual experiences are catalysts that crystallize their desire for psychological growth, but they are not short cuts, nor are they substitutes for the hard work required to achieve that growth. All reputable spiritual traditions warn that if we seek these experiences without being psychologically ready for them, we are taking an enormous risk. Indeed, there are many stories like *The Four Sages Who Entered Paradise* that describe aspiring spiritual masters "who sought to break open the doors of divine awareness, and died or went mad with the onrush of knowledge they were not yet mentally prepared to receive" (Hoffman, 1981, p. 125). This could easily have happened to Sarah had she been unwilling to put her spiritual practices on hold until she regained her psychological balance. Fortunately, she had the courage to rebuild her psychological foundations and thus was able, eventually, to integrate her terrifying spiritual experience in a healthy way. Unfortunately, not all seekers are so wise. Some years ago I watched a colleague become infatuated with other people's spiritual experiences and make excessive use of hallucinogenic drugs in order to induce one in himself. Although he was warned by his meditation teacher that these experiences happen when they are needed, rarely when they are sought, he was unwilling to accept this advice. As my colleague's obsession with spiritual experiences grew, his life began to collapse. His physical and mental health deteriorated, and his increasingly erratic behavior destroyed his marriage and forced him to retire prematurely from an academic position that he loved.

If spiritual awareness is sought precipitously or for the wrong reasons, it can lead to spiritual dementia. Without the proper motivation, a spiritual experience can exacerbate pre-existing cognitive, emotional, and/or moral deficiencies. Indeed, as Michael Murphy (1992) found in his extensive study of mystics and spiritual adepts, "ecstasies, illuminations, and extraordinary powers are no guarantee of lasting goodness or growth" (p. 550). One of the best safeguards is the degree of integrity a person brings to the task of psychological and spiritual growth and the depth of self-knowledge she or he is willing to achieve.

Another safeguard is humility. This is not false modesty or heedless submission, but a deep recognition of the vast, complex, and powerful mystery of Being. A first-hand experience of the multidimensionality of Being can strike terror into the most stalwart of hearts, especially if one lacks a philosophical or psychological context in which to place it. Conversely, a spiritual experience can inflate a person's sense of self-importance and lead to a false belief that he or she is more special than others or has an exclusive corner on the spiritual truth market. Learning to be spiritually intelligent is like learning to swim: one must start slowly, build spiritual "muscles" methodically, and learn how to use them in waters of varying depths. Without humility, one can overestimate one's strength and enter these waters inadequately prepared or for the wrong reasons. When that happens, psychospiritual currents that are unimaginably strong can easily carry one away. As Susan found, "There is a headiness that comes with spiritual experiences but you have to be clear and examine your motives frequently. The universe has a way of slapping you in the face if you don't stay honest."

Susan knew intimately what she was talking about for she, too, had seen what happened to a friend whose pursuit of spiritual awareness became self-destructive and hurtful to people who were close to him. This friend was a physician who had meditated for more than 20 years and could consistently achieve altered states of consciousness. Unfortunately, he did not extend this discipline to his psychological health or personal life. "He was very judgmental," Susan recalled. "He didn't walk his talk.

He used meditation instead of drugs in order to get high. He made lots of spiritual pronouncements that sounded good, but he didn't feel he had to align his behavior with any of them. That was very frightening for me to observe. He drank considerably at times and was very abusive to his body and to other people. I've learned that you can't do that level of meditation and do things like that. Yes, you develop a lot of powers, but without self-awareness things can get ugly pretty fast."

The powers to which Susan referred are another factor that can turn a spiritual experience "upside down." These powers derive from the activation of inner senses that can enable one to perceive and direct phenomena that are too subtle to be detected by the physical senses. Earlier I suggested that these powers are latent in all of us, although we usually experience them sporadically and serendipitously. As one grows in spiritual awareness these powers become more pronounced and can be drawn on deliberately to explore physical reality and the farther reaches of consciousness. Like any tool, however, these powers can be bent to different purposes. They can be used destructively to manipulate other people or to aggrandize oneself, as did Susan's friend, or they can be put to constructive purposes, as Parwati learned to do when she was a shaman's apprentice. Even then, they take some getting used to. "I have found that many people in this country don't want to understand anything about the spiritual world and are scared of people like me," Parwati confessed. "To not be hurt by them psychically or emotionally is really hard. I believe I'm supposed to be a healer and that means I have to be very sensitive in order to pick up on people's energy and needs. But in order to survive in everyday life, I have to close that sensitivity down once in awhile. I never know whether closing myself off will be a good thing or not. I never know how open to be and nobody can tell you. And all this happens every day."

Parwati's experience illustrates a further challenge on the road to spiritual intelligence: the tendency to become acutely, sometimes painfully, sensitive to one's own and others' feelings. Spiritual experiences can magnify the inner senses and dramatically increase a person's capacity to feel. As participants in my study reported, this can enhance empathy and compassion, but it can also lead to a deep sense of isolation. Evelyn Underhill (1911) found that an abiding loneliness was common among the mystics whom she studied, even when their lives were full in other areas. It was common among my informants as well. Although most felt a strong desire to talk about their experiences, particularly in their immediate aftermath, this proved a difficult, sometimes impossible task.

In Chapter One I described some of the difficulties people face in finding language to convey the essence and impact of their spiritual experiences, but the reactions of other people can be equally problematic. Many people in Western culture respond with embarrassment, discomfort, or outright skepticism to experiences that peoples in other cultures, like Parwati's and Maya's, take completely for granted. "It's hard to talk about my experiences outside of Native culture," Maya said. "When I do try to talk about them it feels as if I'm exposing a side of myself that's alien." When Susan tried to describe her encounter with the Medicine Buddha to the Western meditation teachers with whom she was studying at the time, they reacted with a jealousy and hostility that surprised her. "I was told that I couldn't have had this experience because it was only for grand masters and adepts," she recalled. "They said I must have had a breakdown of some sort. This was terribly confusing, and I felt more alone than I had been before."

Spiritual loneliness can become a source of severe psychological stress. Human beings are by nature social creatures and derive a critical sense of well being from their connection to other people. This is particularly true for those who are coping with adverse or traumatic life events. Indeed, the tendency to become physically or mentally ill in the absence of social support is well documented in the literatures of psychology and medicine. Over the past 30 years numerous support groups have helped people cope with a wide variety of life experiences. Unfortunately, there are few places in Western culture where one can turn for help in understanding a spiritual event unless one is a member of an organized religion and one's experience does not conflict with its dogma. But that is not a viable option for all people. Tomas told me he had never discussed his threshold experience before our conversation, not because he didn't want to, but because he didn't know to whom he could confide. "I wish I had access to people I could talk to about this experience in a nonreligious way," he said. "I don't want to talk about the incarnations of Vishnu unless that's a metaphor for what the experience is. I don't want to talk about religion, I don't want to talk about the immortality of the soul, and I certainly don't want to talk about how I was a prince in Atlantis!" Tomas laughed and then grew more serious. "I want to talk existentially about it. Here's this experience and aside from any judgments or weird interpretations that I could put on it, I value it and I want to navigate it."

The support of family and friends can be invaluable when it is available, but it, too, is often missing when spiritual experiences are involved. Although little research has investigated the effects of a spiritual event on members of an individual's support system, psychologist Kenneth Ring (1984) found that near-death experiences placed enormous strain on primary relationships. Several of my informants expressed deep regret that they could not discuss their spiritual experiences with those who were closest to them. "Some of my family members and boyfriends got very angry when I tried to talk about the experiences I described to you," Valerie said. "They didn't understand them and they didn't want to know." According to Ring, "a considerable number of people . . . end up by divorcing their spouses, or at least wanting to" (p. 96).

Dan has no desire to divorce his spouse, but he does wish that spirituality was something he didn't have to hide. Dan's partner of almost 20 years is a physician whom he met when he was preparing to enter graduate school in psychology. Soon after they fell in love, however, his partner wanted to know where Dan stood on the question of spirituality. "That was an important issue for him because of his background," Dan said. "He had been raised in the Catholic Church and found that experience to be extremely traumatizing. He left the church when he was in college and to this day maintains a strong identity as a devout atheist. I shared with him my Christian Science and drug background, the spiritual experiences I told you about, and the fact that I believed in God although I wasn't sure what kind of god. He wanted to debate the subject but I couldn't because for me it isn't a rational issue, it's one of the heart. This difference sometimes causes problems in our relationship because spirituality is one of the few things we can't share."

Yet another challenge on the road to spiritual intelligence is illustrated by the experience of the medieval sage who was so overcome with the beauty of Paradise that he could not bear to return to his earthly life. This is perhaps the most painful dilemma of all. Powerful spiritual experiences make physical reality seem dull and torpid in their wake, like driving a Model-T Ford after piloting an intergalactic starship. One of William James' informants said that his spiritual experiences were the most real experiences of his life. "When they came I was living the fullest, strongest, sanest, deepest life," he said, and he missed that feeling deeply when it inevitably subsided (James, 1902, p. 389). Carl Jung recalled how angry he himself felt and how difficult he was to be around immediately following his spiritual awakening (described in Chapter One).

> In reality, a good three weeks were to pass before I could truly make up my mind to live again. I could not eat because all food repelled me. The view of city and mountains from my sickbed seemed to me like a painted curtain with black holes in it, or a tattered sheet of newspaper full of photographs that meant nothing. Disappointed, I thought, Now I must return to the 'box system' again. . . . Life and the whole world struck me as a prison, and it bothered me beyond all measure. . . . I was tormented and on edge; everything irritated me; everything was too material, too crude and clumsy, terribly limited both spatially and spiritually. It was all an imprisonment, for reasons impossible to divine . . . (1965, pp. 292-295)

I, too, felt bereft and homesick when I returned from the spiritual realms I had visited in 1975, and all too aware of the contrast between where I had been and where I was now. Even though I had not been forced to return, even though I deliberately chose to reenter my physical life, it took several months before I was able to accept my decision fully and reengage with life. During this time I felt completely out of place, and I seesawed between emotional extremes of grief and joy. Tomas had a similar reaction. "I would never under any circumstances want to live the life I was leading before my threshold experience," Tomas said when I asked him about the aftermath of that event. "Nothing would make it worthwhile. It wasn't life. This isn't easy and I wouldn't say that I'm generally happy, but I have moments of happiness. I didn't think I was ever going to feel that. But it does leave me with a tremendous hunger."

The loss that is felt so acutely is for the beauty, serenity, and indescribable vitality of the spiritual realm. As detailed in

Chapters Four and Five, spiritual experiences can impart an extraordinary clarity about the integrity of each individual and the universe. They remind us that everything has meaning and purpose and that all beings are integral to and equal within the whole. It can be wrenching to return to ordinary consciousness after an experience of such intensity and hard to accept, as one of my Buddhist friends is fond of saying, that "before enlightenment the laundry, after enlightenment the laundry." Although the emotional intensity of a spiritual event fades with time, it takes time to absorb the contrast between spiritual and physical reality, and time to remember that physical life is a unique spiritual experience in and of itself. To forget that is to lose all.

Ascending and descending from a spiritual event "in peace" like the fourth medieval sage can take some work, especially if a person does not have access to the kind of support or spiritual tradition that was available to him. Yet even with such support, the aftermath of a spiritual event can include a painful period of psychological adjustment. Generally speaking, the more powerful the experience and/or the more it collides with a person's underlying belief system, the stronger its aftereffects will be. Psychological reactions can be mild to severe and include confusion and disorientation as well as anger and grief. Some people may feel a need for more solitude, especially if they find themselves becoming more cognizant of their own and others' feelings, or more sensitive to subtle energies. Others may need to begin or resume a regular spiritual practice, like yoga, meditation, or contemplative prayer. As long as one gives oneself sufficient space and time to adjust to spiritual insights and to the feelings and awareness evoked by them, the psychological outcome should be quite positive.

Occasionally a person may need professional assistance to come to terms with a spiritual experience. Had Sarah not been able to talk with me about her out-of-body experience, it might have destroyed her psychological balance. Had Valerie not been able to explore the dreams and visions that came to her at critical times, she might not have rebuilt her life after her boyfriend nearly killed her. One must exercise caution in choosing the right helper, however. Spiritual events are rarely discussed in professional forums, and many mental health practitioners are unfamiliar with their psychological impact. Consequently, they can underestimate or misinterpret an experience and its aftermath.

When I attempted to tell my former therapist about my spiritual awakening, I could see her straining to listen objectively. Because she was so competent and because I trusted her so deeply, I was content for a long time to work through what I could with her and remain silent about the role of that event in reshaping my life. But there came a time when I fell into a dark night of the soul that threatened to extinguish all light from my life. Within a nightmarish, 6-month period of time, I suffered a number of major losses. Soon after I completed my doctorate my marriage collapsed; shortly thereafter I miscarried and entered into an early and abrupt menopause. It was extremely hard to find suitable work at the time given the overcrowded condition of my field and, without the safety net of family, I was impoverished and homeless for several months. These hardships frightened my friends, some of whom vanished from my life. For many months I lost all faith in a benevolent and meaningful universe, a loss which for me was devastating. I needed my therapist's help to understand this loss in light of my spiritual experiences, but they ran counter to everything she believed. Because she could not overcome her bias I decided, with sadness, to terminate our relationship, knowing that what I needed and what she could provide had diverged too sharply for me to find solace.

Although mental health professionals are often effective without having had experiences that are similar to their clients, this is not true for spiritual events. A *good enough fit* between helper and client is the basis on which an effective healing relationship is built, but this relationship can never gel if a person feels that she or he must hide a spiritual experience or be thought delusional or neurotic. For this reason I would urge those who seek professional help in the wake of a spiritual event to ask prospective helpers about their spiritual beliefs and experiences. This might cause discomfort for some clinicians because it contradicts the professional detachment they are taught to observe. Yet, most people will not explore the content and meaning of a spiritual experience unless they feel safe, something they will not feel if they sense skepticism or fear from their helper. It takes enormous courage to trust one's inner voice in the face of professional skepticism, but better to listen to that voice than to accept an interpretation that does not fit. Because he works with so many patients who are terminally ill, Dan is often called on to help people integrate spiritual experiences that occur in the dying process. "And sometimes those are hard to be with," he said, "because they're so different. But they're also really significant. Whether they're experiences of being rejoined with friends and family, being blasted into the cosmos, or being reincarnated as an animal, you have to meet people where they're at if you want to help them grow."

Psychologists and therapists with Dan's sensitivity may be hard to find. I have received numerous letters from colleagues who wanted to discuss their own or their patients' spiritual experiences but were afraid to do so publicly. The mainstream psychological community often reacts negatively to spirituality, and no one wants to have his or her competence questioned. Word of mouth, ecumenical centers for spiritual development, hospices, and associations for near-death experiences are good sources to tap when looking for competent and sympathetic professional advice.

Whether a person wants or needs professional help to integrate a spiritual experience, Susan's advice to "read copiously" is excellent. There are many fine sources of spiritual and metaphysical information, and myriad descriptions of spiritual events. A number are listed in the Bibliography. Reading about other people's experiences can help a person achieve greater insight into his or her own experience. Remember, however, that all experiences are indelibly colored by people's cultural, educational, and religious backgrounds, and that no one interpretation can be generalized to all. Because I am scientifically oriented, it makes sense that my spiritual awakening would involve equations, but they would have little relevance for Tony, who is more artistic and thinks in different terms. As compelling as another person's experience might seem, the best course of action is to think for oneself.

It is also important to remember that spiritual experiences serve unique psychological needs and that different needs determine different paths. There is no one or right way to attain spiritual awareness. Indeed, "what is good medicine for one may be poison for another" (Basu, 1983, p. 33). I believe that there are many valid routes to spiritual intelligence, although what is considered "right" from one perspective might be regarded as heresy from another. According to some teachers, spiritual awareness requires one to lose one's sense of self; other teachers argue that to do so is both foolhardy and unnecessary. Some teachers say that "the choice of path is determined by the specific qualification of the candidate in question, and not by any inherent quality in it" (Basu, 1983, p. 391). Others believe that paths are graded, with one being inherently superior or inferior to another. Some allege that one must attain a certain level of growth before aspiring to the next, but others hold that spiritual growth has no fixed endpoint or stations on the way. Perhaps one day we will have enough knowledge to be able to recommend different paths to different people with a high degree of confidence. Until then, it is incumbent on each of us to pay close attention to the changing demands of our growth, listen to our intuition and inner voices, and proceed accordingly.

Finally, a person must be willing to evaluate the effects of spiritual experiences over time. "I do believe that the Universe can play with you," Maya reflected. "You don't want to be gullible or seduced by anything. You always want to be aware and look to yourself." Spiritual experiences can potentiate psychological health, but they do not shield us from the twists and turns of life. Indeed, sometimes they seem to intensify life's challenges. "I'd like to believe that we can achieve true, deep spiritual understanding without an enormous amount of suffering," Susan reflected, "but I really don't think we can. I think that's part of the path. Someone gave me a Scott Peck daily calendar with little phrases on it, and one said something like 'For people seeking spiritual growth, basically be warned, you're going to endure enormous suffering and you'll be called upon to do things that you could not imagine having to do or having to sacrifice.' That's as close as I've found to what I've experienced, and I haven't found many people who haven't also paid a huge price for coming to a deep understanding."

The road to spiritual intelligence is arduous and requires that we be conscious, aware, and psychologically present on a daily basis. This task is easy for no one, particularly for those of us who live in frenetic Western cultures. But as Michael Murphy argued, if "we do not accommodate the many powers in which we are secretly rooted, they come to us anyway, as physical sickness, depression, obsession, or unexpected epiphanies that disrupt our everyday functioning" (1992, p. 560). They come as the myriad manifestations of spiritual dementia with which we are all too familiar: the disintegration of the social fabric, violence, child abuse, alcoholism, and drug addiction. They come as religious and ethnic warfare, overpopulation, and the overwhelming socioeconomic and environmental problems that fill many with despair. This is not to suggest that spiritual intelligence would transform humanity into a race of saints or superheroes, but it would help us to remember that each of us is here for a reason and that our capacity for growth is limitless. Like Tony, it would help us pay as much attention to our spiritual needs as we do to our bodies and minds and make psychospiritual fitness an integral part of our daily lives. Like Maya, it would help us learn to live life deliberately rather than to endure it passively, and to allow sorrow and joy to peacefully coexist. Like Dan and Parwati, it would enable us to heal our wounds and use that health to help others. Like Tomas, it would enlarge our capacity for empathy and compassion so that we do not succumb to rage or despair, or close ourselves down and feel nothing at all. Like Susan and Alex, it would help us see affliction as an instrument of awakening that can set us back on track rather than derail us. Like Valerie, it would help us remember that we all have important parts to sing in the symphony of life, no matter how afraid or unworthy we might occasionally feel. And like Megan, it would help us realize that spiritual intelligence can be found in the most tragic of circumstances and help us transform those events into creativity and greater awareness.

How might spiritual intelligence shape humankind's collective future? No one can say. At the very least we might realize that individual differences are both enriching and irrelevant, and thereby achieve more tolerance and respect for all life forms. We might begin to harness the extraordinary powers that are latent in our minds and to use them to bring balance and perspective to our burgeoning technological capabilities. We might discover new methods for physical and psychological healing that are less costly, more efficacious, and available to all rather than some. We might also evolve a new paradigm of morality that would enable us to live in greater harmony with all beings and simultaneously lessen our individual and collective terror of death. No matter where spiritual intelligence might lead us, one thing is clear: the mystical is in the moment and we live there all the time. Like Dorothy in the Land of Oz, we have only to look within to find our way home.

CHAPTER SEVEN

The Next
Frontier

Hubble pointed at one of the emptiest parts of the sky, focused on a region the size of a grain of sand held at arm's length, and found layer upon layer of galaxies as far as its eye could see.
　　—Robert Williams, the Hubble Deep Field Team, and NASA

If humankind were able to create an instrument like the Hubble telescope that allowed us to probe the inner regions of our own selves, what might we see? According to the instruments we currently have available—the perceptions of people of all ages and in all eras who have had spiritual experiences—inner space is no emptier than the regions of outer space now visible through Hubble's lens. Like deep space itself, we are "grains of sand held at arm's length," and within all of us lie galaxies of consciousness that are bursting with intelligence and life. The task before us is to use this awareness in the service of our greater well being.

Some people already know how to do this. There are shamans and healers the world over who can perceive subtle energies and control physiological functions in ways that traditional Western sciences cannot explain. There are individuals who can alter their state of consciousness at will and use their dreams and inner senses to explore both the physical and spiritual realms. There are ordinary people who demonstrate an extraordinary capacity for goodness—what Buddhists call "loving kindness" and Native Americans a "moist heart"—and who use this capacity to serve their own and other species. There are people who endure conditions of incomprehensible trauma and despair, and whose awareness, tolerance, compassion, and resilience are strengthened, not diminished, by those experiences. And there are some, like the great prophets and spiritual teachers who partake regularly in the "supreme experience, inexpressible in human tongues, [which] is everywhere one and the same" (Basu, 1983, p. 355), who are exemplars of exceptional health and well being.

Are these individuals born with an extremely high degree of spiritual intelligence, just as some people are born with extraordinary aptitudes for music, athletics, or artistic pursuits? Can spiritual intelligence, like other forms of intelligence, be developed over time with practice and intent? How does spiritual intelligence express itself in different populations? Would a spiritually intelligent person be recognizable in any culture or era? Can one be "profoundly gifted" or "profoundly delayed" in spiritual terms? Why are some people driven to be psychologically and spiritually well while others could care less? How could spiritual intelligence become more accessible to more people more of the time?

These are questions that some of us in the field of giftedness have begun to study in earnest. They are not easy questions to answer nor are they new. Indeed, spiritual seekers throughout the ages have asked them, in one form or another, of all who would listen. What is different about our era is that more of us seem to be listening than ever before. And, for the first time, philosophers, physicists, artists, and psychologists, among others, are engaging in multidisciplinary conversations about consciousness and spirituality at secular universities and private think tanks throughout the world. Perhaps, wittingly or not, humankind is embarking on a change in its collective consciousness that will dwarf any that has come before.

Revolutions in human consciousness are not uncommon. The Cartesian revolution, which promulgated the belief that "there exists nothing in the whole of nature that cannot be explained in terms of purely corporeal causes," ushered in the Age of Reason and supplanted a theological belief system that had dominated the social and intellectual life of Western Europe for almost 700 years. In doing so, it opened the way for the industrial, scientific, and technological revolutions that have so radically reshaped the lives of most inhabitants of Earth.

Changes in major belief systems do not occur overnight, for individuals or for groups. As one paradigm gives way to another there is always a period of overlap and instability. Grand inquisitors were trying and executing people for witchcraft when the scientific revolution was in its infancy, and there are still lethal clashes over issues of dogma and heresy between and among religious groups. It took hundreds of years for people to accept Copernicus' discovery that the earth revolves around the sun and hundreds more for the first telescope, built by Galileo, to metamorphose into the Hubble, built by NASA. Microbes and organ transplants were once real only in the imaginations of science fiction writers, as were the means of mass communication, mass transportation, and mass computation that we take for granted today. The innovations of this century, the comforts of modern life—all have evolved from humankind's romance with reason. But like any powerful idea, we too must evolve or be suffocated by the weight of our own history.

Perhaps our species is finally becoming mature enough to move beyond the confines of Reason and toward a recognition that nothing exists in the whole of nature that can *only* be explained in purely corporeal terms. Perhaps we will find new ways to bridge the gap that has artificially divided the physical from the spiritual, without fanning the flames of religious or scientific intolerance and persecution. Perhaps as we find new ways to understand the underlying processes of consciousness, we will find new ways to eradicate the social and environmental challenges left in the Cartesian wake. Perhaps the Age of Reason will evolve into the Age of Consciousness, to the benefit of us all.

In that new frontier, spiritual intelligence would be as necessary a navigational skill as reading, writing, and personal computing are to the modern world. To repeat what I said in

Chapter Three, spiritual intelligence is not religiosity or piety, the practice of any particular spiritual discipline, or adherence to any particular theology or creed. It is, instead, the ability to explore systematically the spiritual dimensions of our own being and to infuse what we learn into every aspect of our lives.

I am convinced by my experiences and by my research that spiritual intelligence is not a gift that is bestowed on a select few, but an innate potential that can be activated by anyone who chooses to do so. Choice, not chance, is the key that unlocks this potential. Spiritual intelligence can only be achieved by expanding our psychological breadth and depth, living more deliberately, and functioning more wholly as individuals and in the world. Further, one must choose to perceive everyone and everything as more than meets the waking eye and choose to consciously align one's behavior with that awareness.

Spiritual experiences are the catalysts that propel us toward this new frontier because they give us first-hand knowledge of "the enormous, rich, complex, and unknown life within us of which we are seldom or never aware (Zilboorg, 1941, p. 488). Does this mean that one experience is necessarily more "spiritual" than another? I believe that the spiritual, like beauty, is in the eye of the beholder. Indeed, if "all that is is holy," as Meister Eckhart said, then everyone and everything is an aspect of the Divine. Spiritual intelligence enables us to see this.

Learning to *see* rather than to see is crucial to this frame of mind. It is a difference that the Yaqui sorcerer Don Juan went to great pains to explain to his reluctant apprentice, Carlos Castenada. *Seeing* is like contemplating a *Magic Eye* picture and learning to see beyond the illusion of its two dimensionality. It takes time to see depth in what initially appears to be surface flatness, and a willingness to believe that it is there, even before the third dimension emerges. It takes practice to bring this dimension into focus and effort to bring one's focus back when it inevitably fades.

The first *Sight*—or spiritual awakening—that one has is usually serendipitous and usually dramatic. Because most people live at a distance from their inner selves, it often takes a spiritual shock to attract our attention. Sometimes this shock takes a positive form. As Buddhist philosopher Chogyam Trungpa (1985) explained,

Everyone has experienced a wind of energy or power in their lives. For example, athletes feel a surge of energy when they are engaged in their sport. Or a person may experience a torrent of love or passion for another human being to whom he or she is attracted. . . . Normally we think that this energy comes from a definite source or has a particular cause. We associate it with the situation in which we become so energized. . . . It actually comes from nowhere, but is always there. It is the energy of basic goodness. (pp. 84-85)

But a shock from this source of energy does not always feel good. In my experience, many people would never open their minds to their spiritual dimensions were it not for unhappy events. Megan's awakening came when her son was killed and she accompanied him through the threshold of death. Susan, Maya, and Parwati first opened their eyes to their spiritual dimensions whey they suffered serious illnesses. Valerie's dangerous life on the streets, the break-up of Tony's relationship, and Alex's and my major depressions drove each of us to seek new visions in the depths of ourselves.

Whether it is triggered by positive or negative events, a spiritual awakening always "bears in some sort the stamp of [the individual's] uniqueness. . . . For there is an element of mystery in each soul which no amount of analysis, scientific or metaphysical, is ever able to reduce or solve, and it is this element which determines the specific character of the enjoyment which the soul feels in communion with the Divine" (Basu, 1983, pp. 1-2). I often wonder whether the more spiritually intelligent we become, the less we need psychological shocks to wake us up. I suspect that the less willing we are to *see* and enjoy the more subtle means of divine communication, the more clamorous those means become.

Whereas the first *sight* often happens by chance, spiritual intelligence does not. A spiritual awakening is a powerful signal that the "glass" of consciousness in which we are swimming has grown too small for the persons we are becoming and that we must move beyond its borders or risk suffocation. Spiritual intelligence is the ongoing, deliberate, sometimes difficult process of psychological expansion. We learn to swim in deeper waters of consciousness by breaking down and breaking through the psychological boundaries that limit our perceptions of physical existence. These lessons can come from crisis or contemplation, but their insights must be revisited on a regular basis or we rapidly fall back to sleep. The psychospiritual "muscles" that make spiritual intelligence viable can be kept fit only through regular use. This is rarely easy in contemporary lives that are rich in distractions, but spiritual exercise is as necessary to the psyche as physical exercise is to the body.

Another means toward spiritual intelligence is learning to listen to one's inner voice. The private languages that we speak to ourselves are symbolic, idiosyncratic, and tailored to our underlying beliefs about existence. At first this inner voice might seem faint or nonexistent, but by paying close attention to dreams, feelings, reflections, and everyday experiences, we can decode its messages on a reliable basis. In my experience, the inner voice is the only compass that can safely guide a person through an expanding inner universe. Once again, choice and effort are crucial to success.

There are many methods that can help people to develop their spiritual intelligence. Some are ancient and include spiritual disciplines such as yoga, meditation, and contemplative prayer. Others are more recent and include psychotherapy, lucid dreaming, neurofeedback, and hemispheric synchronization. Undoubtedly, new consciousness technologies will be added to this repertoire over time. No matter what method one chooses, it should be a method that one enjoys practicing. I do not say this lightly. Not only is the best form of exercise the one that we will do (as all health professionals advise), but as Thomas Aquinas said

> If we become spiritual only by an imperative issuing from reason and will, virtue is in some way forced. . . . It would proceed with repugnance and frustration that leads to sadness instead of blossoming into a state of delight. (quoted in Fox, 1981, p. 197)

I believe that the pursuit of spiritual intelligence need not be a grim process nor can it best be attained through self-punishment or unhealthy forms of self-denial. To me, the point of developing spiritual intelligence is neither perfection nor loss of self, but a greater sense of wonder and joy in the process and progress of being. Both die quickly in the face of rigidity.

Regardless of the method one uses to develop spiritual intelligence, one must exercise caution and good judgment. If we mistake the tool for the transformation, our progress will stall. There is an old story about a young monk that illustrates this dilemma. At a critical point in the monk's spiritual development he was sent from the monastery by his teacher into the larger world to discover for himself a truth about life. The monk wandered for a time and eventually came to a river where he stopped to rest. Gazing at the distant coastline, he decided to fulfill his master's assignment by learning to walk on the water. Many years later the now middle-aged monk successfully reached the other side and returned to the monastery, expecting to receive his master's approbation. Instead, the master shook his head with sadness and told him he had wasted his time. "For only a penny you could have paid the ferry man to row you across the river," he said. "How much more you might have learned if you had."

As important as effort, commitment, and good judgment are to spiritual intelligence, "maturity is essential to the transaction" (Bulka, 1970, p 7). It takes both psychological and spiritual maturity to accept the idea that existence is not accidental. I often remind my clients and myself that "no one is here for a vacation." By this I mean that no one is a passive observer who must endure a meaningless life and then fade into oblivion. Each of us is an active partner in an ongoing, reciprocal relationship with our own selves, and each of us is the playwright, director, set designer, hero, villain, and audience of those selves. Further, each of us is a vivid and unique expression of a larger, multidimensional reality with which we interact, consciously and unconsciously, on a moment-by-moment basis. The mature choice is to become more conscious.

Maturity also demands that *all* experiences be seen within the broader context of a person's life and examined with a thoroughness that does not avoid uncomfortable truths. If Valerie is not committed to maintaining her sobriety, alcoholism will strip her dreams and visions of their curative power. If Maya stops learning how to live after years of trying to die, her Thanksgiving insight will be lost in the chaos of inevitable despair. If Susan were not committed to working through the aftermath of the emotional, physical, and sexual abuse heaped on her by her family and her ex-husband, her encounter with the Medicine Buddha might have triggered a psychological breakdown rather than a breakthrough. Spiritual experiences are not substitutes for the hard work of healing. The importance to spiritual intelligence of resolving unfinished psychological business cannot be overstated.

The real work of psychospiritual growth always begins after the emotional intensity of an awakening fades. In an increasingly digital world where speed is rarely fast enough, the temptation to succumb to "a narrowing of vision, a desire for instant ecstasy, instant salvation . . . the quest for the correct method, the right mantra, the short cut which brings insight" (Leech, 1985, p. 20) can be intense. But there are no short cuts to spiritual intelligence. As Richard Woods said, "all human persons are at bottom mystics" because all human persons are learning how to live (1981, p. 426). Spiritual intelligence is a frame of mind and a way of life that can only be cultivated over time in a careful and disciplined way. It can develop in delight and bring more joy and self-fulfillment into a person's life, but it is not a permanent state of bliss. It is a state of awareness, one that is an ongoing effort of will rather than of feeling. It is a state of *not knowing* that calls for tolerance and respect for what Buddhists call *Beginner's Mind.* The old adage—that the more we know the more we know we don't know—is perhaps more true of spiritual intelligence than of any other frame of mind. Without a mature respect for one's cosmic status as a perpetual student, spiritual intelligence gives way to spiritual dementia or disillusionment.

A mature respect for one's status as a student allows us to approach our inner selves with curiosity, respect, and trust, the attitudes that Megan has learned to adopt when she approaches the stones she plans to carve. These attitudes enable us to ask ourselves, with confidence, for experiences that will further our understanding. Then, in Maya's words, "we have to be willing to get out of the way." The answers we seek always come but we have to actively wait for them with what the I Ching describes as "the inner certainty of reaching the goal" (1950, p. 24)." As Alex discovered, "the Universe is really responsive to all us little preschoolers," but its timing is unpredictable and its responses only come when we are psychologically ready to handle them.

There is a saying among psychologists that each child in a family has a different set of parents. In other words, each person experiences a psychological reality that is uniquely his or her own. Much as we might wish it otherwise, the answers to our most pressing questions—be they psychological, emotional, or spiritual—must come from within. Each of us must be the final arbiter of our experience. This does not mean that teachers are irrelevant or unnecessary. Other people can and must at times guide us through ourselves. But only we can live there.

Finally, maturity requires us to be open selectively to spiritual experiences and careful not to deceive or fool ourselves. Paradoxically, this requires the willingness to doubt or to bring what my colleague Clark Johnson (personal communication, January 1999) calls "constructive skepticism" to an examination of any spiritual insight or event. It also requires a healthy respect for fear. Most people are afraid of the unknown, and that includes their own selves. This primal fear may be why spiritual awakenings catch so many people unaware. Constructive fear, like constructive skepticism, helps us know when to advance and when to retreat. As the Four Sages story so poignantly reminds us, it is always possible to go too far too fast. Spiritual intelligence may ask us to boldly go where few have gone before, but it never asks us to leave our good sense behind.

Toward the end of the spiritual experience with which I opened this book, I sat among my ethereal friends, trying to understand the mess we humans were making in our small sector of the cosmos. As I bemoaned the fact that things were much worse than we had thought they could be, my friends smiled at me with immense kindness but equally vast indulgence. "Ah," they said, "you have only forgotten that you are all involved in an ongoing experiment in consciousness. You are fully capable of reaching a new level of awareness. You just have to want to."

As I mature as a person and as a psychologist, I am beginning to understand more fully the meaning of their words. Pelagius argued in the 5th century CE that "the secret of the state of creative being lies in achieving a balance between inner revelation and outward manifestation" (quoted in Fox, 1981, p. 181). Evelyn Underhill (1911) described this as "remaking our characters about newer and higher centers of life" (p. 446). I think of it as *riding the windhorse* with grace and integrity. No matter what metaphor one employs, no one can reach a new level of awareness without learning to see the sacred at work in all that exists, including oneself. This is not narcissism or egocentrism. On the contrary, the more aware we become of the sacred within us, the more seriously we take our connection to all other beings and the more responsibly we behave in our personal and community lives.

This, then, is how I have come to understand the passage from the Gnostic Gospels that has haunted me for so long. If we bring forth that which is within us—our spiritual intelligence—what we bring forth will save us. If we do not bring forth that which is within us, our apathy and ignorance will destroy us. The choice is always—and only—our own. For better or worse, we are in our own hands.

References

Allman, L.S., De La Rocha, O., Elkins, D.N., & Weathers, R.S. (1992). Psychotherapists' attitudes toward clients reporting mystical experiences. *Psychotherapy, 29*, 564-569.

Anthony, E.J., & Cohler, B.J. (Eds.). (1987). *The invulnerable child.* New York: Guilford.

Asrani, U.A. (1972). The psychology of mysticism. In J. White (Ed.), *The highest state of consciousness* (pp. 225-239). New York: Anchor Books.

Arus, R., Davis, H.T., & Stuewer, R.H. (Eds.). (1983). *Springs of scientific creativity: Essays on founders of modern science.* Minneapolis: University of Minnesota Press.

Asante, M.K. (1984). The African American mode of transcendence. *Journal of Transpersonal Psychology, 16*, 167-177.

Baruss, I., & Moore, R.J. (1992). Measurement of beliefs about consciousness and reality. *Psychological Reports, 71*, 59-64.

Basu, S. (1983). *Some mystics of modern India; Volumes I and II.* Taiwan: The Orient Cultural Service.

Batson, C.D., & Ventis, W.L (1982). *The religious experience: A social-psychological perspective.* New York: Oxford University Press.

Beloff, J. (1975). The study of the paranormal as an educative experience. *Parapsychology Review, 6,* 8-11.

Bennett, G. (1987). *Traditions of belief: Women, folklore, and the supernatural today.* London: Penguin Books.

Bloomfield, H.H. (1980). Transcendental meditation as an adjunct to therapy. In S. Boorstein (Ed.), *Transpersonal psychotherapy* (pp. 123-140). Palo Alto, CA: Science & Behavior Books.

Boorstein, S. (Ed.). (1980). *Transpersonal psychotherapy.* Palo Alto, CA: Science & Behavior Books.

Brophy, T. G. (1999). *The mechanism demands a mysticism: An exploration of spirit, matter, and physics.* Blue Hill, ME: Medicine Bear Publishing.

Bucke, R.M. (1972). From self to cosmic consciousness. In J. White (Ed.), *The highest state of consciousness* (pp. 79-93). New York: Anchor Books.

Bulka, R.P. (1970). *Mystics and medics: A comparison of mystical and psychotherapeutic encounters.* New York: Human Sciences Press.

Bunge, M. (1962). *Intuition and science.* Englewood Cliffs, NJ: Prentice-Hall.

Capra, F. (1975). *The Tao of physics: An exploration of the parallels between modern physics and Eastern mysticism.* Berkeley, CA: Shambhala.

Castenada, C. (1985). *Teachings of Don Juan: A Yaqui way of knowledge.* New York: Pocket Books.

Castenada, C. (1991). *Tales of power.* New York: Pocket Books.

Clarke, A. C. (1953). *Childhood's end.* New York: Harcourt, Brace & World.

Delmonte, M.M. (1980). Personality characteristics and regularity of meditation. *Psychological Reports, 46,* 703, 712.

Dugan, T.F., & Coles, R. (1989). *The child in our times: Studies in the development of resiliency.* New York: Brunner/Mazel.

Emmons, R.A. (1999). *The psychology of ultimate concerns: Motivation and spirituality in personality.* New York: Guilford.

Feldman, D.H. (1986). *Nature's gambit: Child prodigies and the development of human potential.* New York: Basic Books.

Fite, R.C. (1981). A psychological study of persons reporting mystical experience. *Dissertation Abstracts International, 42*(2503B).

Flach, F. (1988). *Resilience: Discovering a new strength at times of stress.* New York: Fawcett Columbine.

Fling, S., Thomas, A., & Gallaher, M. (1981). Participant characteristics and the effects of two types of meditation vs. quiet sitting. *Journal of Clinical Psychology, 37,* 784-790.

Fox, M. (Ed.). (1981). *Western spirituality: Historical roots, ecumenical routes.* Santa Fe, NM: Bear & Company.

Freud, S. (1935). *Autobiography* (J. Strachey, trans.). New York: Norton.

Friedman, H.L., & MacDonald, D.A. (1997). Toward a working definition of transpersonal assessment. *Journal of Transpersonal Psychology, 29,* 105-122.

Friedman, N. (1990). *Bridging science and spirit: Common elements in David Bohm's physics, the perennial philosophy, and Seth.* St. Louis, MO: Living Lake Books.

Gardner, H. (1993). *Frames of mind: The theory of multiple intelligences.* New York: Basic Books.

Garmezy, N., & Tellegen, A. (1984). Studies of stress-resistant children: Methods, variables, and preliminary findings. In F.J. Morrison, C. Lord, & D.P. Keating (Eds.), *Applied developmental psychology* (pp. 231-283). Orlando, FL: Academic Press.

Getzells, J.W., & Csikszentmihalyi, M. (1976). *The creative vision: A longitudinal study of problem finding in art.* New York: Wiley.

Goleman, D. (1976). Meditation and consciousness: An Asian approach to mental health. *American Journal of Psychotherapy, 30,* 41-54.

Greeley, A. (1974). *Ecstasy: A way of knowing.* Englewood Cliffs, NJ: Prentice-Hall.

Greeley, A. (1987). Mysticism goes mainstream. *American Health,* Jan/Feb, 47-49.

Greyson, B., & Stevenson, I. (1980). The phenomenology of near-death experiences. *American Journal of Psychiatry, 137*(10), 1193-1196.

Hay, D., & Morisy, A. (1978). Reports of ecstatic, paranormal, or religious experience in Great Britain and the United States: A comparison of trends. *Journal for the Scientific Study of Religion, 17,* 255-268.

Herman, J.L. (1992). *Trauma and recovery.* New York: Basic Books.

Higgins, G.O. (1994). *Resilient adults: Overcoming a cruel past.* San Francisco: Jossey-Bass.

Hjelle, L.A. (1977). Transcendental meditation and psychological health. *Perceptual and Motor Skills, 39,* 632-638.

Hoffman, E. (1981). *The way of splendor: Jewish mysticism and modern psychology.* Boulder, CO: Shambhala.

Hollingworth, L.S. (1914). Variability as related to sex differences in achievement: A critique. *American Journal of Sociology, 19,* 510-530.

Hollingworth, L.E. (1926). *Gifted children: Their nature and nurture.* New York: Macmillan.

Hood, R., Jr. (1975). The construction and preliminary validation of a measure of reported mystical experience. *Journal for the Scientific Study of Religion, 14,* 29-41.

The I Ching Book of Changes. (1950). R. Wilhelm & C.F. Baines (trans.). Princeton, NJ: Princeton University Press.

James, W. (1902). *The varieties of religious experience.* New York: Modern Library.

Jewkes, S., & Baruss, I. (in press). Personality correlates of beliefs about consciousness and reality, *Advanced Development.*

Johnson, K.P. (1998). *Edgar Cayce in context: The readings, truth and fiction.* Albany: State University of New York Press.

Jung, C.G. (1958). *The undiscovered self.* Boston: Little Brown.

Jung, C.G. (1965). *Memories, dreams, reflections.* New York: Vintage Books.

Keutzer, C.S. (1978). Whatever turns you on: Triggers to transcendent experience. *Journal of Humanistic Psychology, 18,* 77-80.

King, U. (1980). *Towards a new mysticism: Teilhard de Chardin and eastern religions.* London: William Collins Sons & Co. Ltd.

Klass, D., & & Gordon, A. (1978). Varieties of transcending experience at death: A videotape based study. *Omega, 9,* 19-35.

Kors, A.C., & Peters, E. (Eds.). (1972). *Witchcraft in Europe 1100-1700: A documentary history.* Philadelphia: University of Pennsylvania Press.

Krippner, S. (1972). Altered states of consciousness. In J. White (Ed.), *The highest state of consciousness* (pp. 1-5). Garden City, NY: Anchor.

Kuhn, T.S. (1970). *The structure of scientific revolutions* (2nd ed.). Chicago: University of Chicago Press.

Leech, K. (1985). *Experiencing God: Theology as spirituality.* San Francisco: Harper & Row.

LeShan, L. (1974). *How to meditate.* Toronto: Bantam Books.

LeShan, L. (1976). *Alternate realities.* New York: M. Evans.

LeShan, L. (1990). *The dilemma of psychology: A psychologist looks at his troubled profession.* New York: Dutton.

Lester, J.T. (1983). Wrestling with the self on Mount Everest. *Journal of Humanistic Psychology, 23,* 31-41.

Ludwig, A.M. (1969). Altered states of consciousness. In C. Tart (Ed.), *Altered states of consciousness* (pp. 11-24). New York: Doubleday.

Lukoff, D., & Everest, H.C. (1985). The myths in mental illness. *Journal of Transpersonal Psychology, 17,* 123-153.

MacDonald, D.A. (1997). *The development of a comprehensive factor analytically derived measure of spirituality and its relationship to psychological functioning.* Unpublished doctoral dissertation, University of Windsor, Canada.

MacDonald, D.A., LeClair, L., Holland, C.J., Alter, A., & Friedman, H.L. (1995). A survey of measures of transpersonal constructs. *Journal of Transpersonal Psychology, 27,* 171-235.

MacDonald, D.A., Tsagarakis, C.I., & Holland, C.J. (1994). Validation of a measure of transpersonal self-concept and its relationship to Jungian and five-factor model conceptions of personality. *Journal of Transpersonal Psychology, 26,* 175-202.

Maslow, A. (1970). *Religion, values, and peak experiences.* New York: Penguin Books.

Mathes, E.W., Zevon, M.A., Roter, P.M., & Joerger, S.M. (1982). Peak experiences tendencies scale: Development and theory testing. *Journal of Humanistic Psychology, 22,* 92-108.

McGaa, E. (1992). *Rainbow tribe: Ordinary people journeying on the red road.* San Francisco: HarperSanFrancisco.

Mitchell, E.D. (Ed.). (1974). *Psychic exploration: A challenge for science.* New York: G.P. Putnam's Sons.

Monroe, R.A. (1977). *Journeys out of the body.* Garden City, NY: Anchor.

Monroe, R.A. (1985). *Far journeys.* Garden City, NY: Doubleday.

Montgomery, R. (1934). Anthropology and the abnormal. *Journal of General Psychology, 10,* 59-80.

Morse, M. (1990). *Closer to the light: Learning from the near death experiences of children.* New York: Ivy.

Morse, M. (1994). *Parting visions: Pre-death visions and spiritual experiences.* New York: Villard Books.

Murphy, L.B. (1987). Further reflections on resilience. In E.J. Anthony & B.J. Cohler (Eds.), *The invulnerable child* (pp. 84-105). New York: Guilford.

Murphy, M. (1992). *The future of the body: Explorations into the further evolution of human nature.* Los Angeles: Jeremy P. Tarcher.

Nash, C. (1976). Medical parapsychology. In R.A. White (Ed.), *Surveys in parapsychology: Reviews of the literature with updated bibliographies* (pp. 120-138). Metuchen, NJ: Scarecrow Press.

Noble, K. D. (1984). Psychological health and the experience of transcendence (Doctoral dissertation, University of Washington, 1984). *Dissertation Abstracts International*, 45(5B), 1576.

Noble, K.D. (1987). Psychological health and the experience of transcendence. *The Counseling Psychologist, 15*, 601-614.

Noble, K. (1994). *The sound of a silver horn: Reclaiming the heroism in contemporary women's lives.* New York: Fawcett Columbine.

Noyes R., & Slymen, D.J. (1979). The subjective response to life-threatening danger. *Omega, 9*, 313-321.

Nuernberger, P. (1994). The structure of mind and its resources. In M.E. Miller & S.R. Cook-Greuter (Eds.), *Transcendence and mature thought in adulthood* (pp. 89-115). Boston: Rowman & Littlefield.

Nystul, M.S., & Garde, M. (1977). The self-concepts of regular transcendental meditators, drop-out meditators, and non-meditators. *Journal of Psychology*, 15-18.

Osis, K., & Haroldsson, E. (1977). *At the hour of death.* New York: Avon Books.

Pagels, E. (1979). *The Gnostic gospels.* New York: Vintage Books.

Pahnke, W.N. (1972). Drugs and mysticism. In J. White (Ed.), *The highest state of consciousness* (pp. 257-277). New York: Anchor Books.

Prince, R.H., & Savage, C. (1972). The mystical states and the concept of regression. In J. White (Ed.), *The highest state of consciousness* (pp. 114-134). New York: Anchor Books.

Puharich, A. (1974). *The sacred mushroom: Key to the door of eternity.* Garden City, NY: Doubleday.

Puharich, H.K. (1974). Psychic research and the healing process. In E. Mitchell (Ed.), *Psychic exploration: A challenge for science* (pp. 333-348). New York: G.P. Putnam's Sons.

Radin, D.I. (1997). *The conscious universe: The scientific truth of psychic phenomena.* New York: HarperEdge.

Ring, K. (1980). *Life at death: A scientific investigation of the near-death experience.* New York: Coward, McCann, & Geoghegan.

Ring, K. (1984). *Heading toward omega: In search of the meaning of the near death experience.* New York: William Morrow.

Sabom, M. (1982). *Recollections of death.* New York: Harper & Row.

Schwartz, H. (1993). *Gabriel's palace: Jewish mystical tales.* New York: Oxford University Press.

Shapiro, D., Jr. (1980). *Meditation: Self-regulation strategy and altered state of consciousness.* New York: Aldine.

Sheldrake, R. (1988). *The presence of the past: Morphic resonance and the habits of nature.* New York: Times Books.

Simonton, O.C. (1978). *Getting well again.* New York: Bantam Books.

Spanos, N.P., Steggles, S., Rodtke-Bodorik, H.L., & Rivers, S.M. (1979). Non-analytic, hypnotic susceptibility and psychological well-being in trained meditators and nonmeditators. *Journal of Abnormal Psychology, 88,* 85-87.

Stevenson, I. (1974). *Twenty cases suggestive of reincarnation.* Charlottesville: University Press of Virginia.

Stevenson, I. (1987). *Children who remember previous lives: A question of reincarnation.* Charlottesville: University Press of Virginia.

Stone, M. (1978). *When God was a woman.* San Diego, CA: Harcourt Brace Jovanovich.

Targ, R., & Puthoff, H.E. (1977). *Mind-reach: Scientists look at psychic ability.* New York: Delacorte.

Targ, R., & Katra, J. (1998). *Miracles of mind: Exploring nonlocal consciousness and spiritual healing.* Novato, CA: New World Library.

Tart. C.T. (Ed.). (1969). *Altered states of consciousness.* New York: Doubleday.

Tart, C.T. (Ed.). (1975). *Transpersonal psychologies.* New York: Harper & Row.

Thomas, L.E., & Cooper, P.E. (1980). Incidence and psychological correlates of intense spiritual experiences. *Journal of Transpersonal Psychology 12,* 75-85.

Tompkins, P., & Bird, C. (1973). *The secret life of plants.* New York: Harper & Row.

Trungpa, C. (1985). *Shambhala: The sacred path of the warrior.* Boston: Shambhala Publications.

Tuchman, B.W. (1978). *A distant mirror: The calamitous 14th century.* New York: Ballantine Books.

Underhill, E. (1911). *Mysticism.* New York: E.P. Dutton.

Walters, J., & Gardner, H. (1986). The crystallizing experience: Discovering an intellectual gift. In R.J. Sternberg & J.E. Davidson (Eds.), *Conceptions of giftedness* (pp. 306-331). Cambridge: Cambridge University Press.

Wapnick, K. (1972). Mysticism and schizophrenia. In J. White (Ed.), *The highest state of consciousness* (pp. 153-174). New York: Anchor Books.

Weber, R. (1986). *Dialogues with scientists and sages: The search for unity.* London: Routledge & Kegan Paul.

Weil, A. (1972). *The natural mind.* Boston: Houghton Mifflin.

White, J. (Ed.). (1972). *The highest state of consciousness.* New York: Anchor.

Wolman, B. (Ed.). (1977). *Handbook of parapsychology.* New York: Van Nostrand Reinhold.

Woods, R. J. (1981). Mysticism, Protestantism, and ecumenism: The spiritual theology of William Ernest Hocking. In M. Fox (Ed.), *Western spirituality: Historical roots, ecumenical routes* (pp. 414-435). Santa Fe, NM: Bear & Company.

Wuthnow, R. (1978). Peak experiences: Some empirical tests. *Journal of Humanistic Psychology, 18,* 59-75.

Yinger, J.M. (1957). *Religion, society, and the individual: An introduction to the sociology of religion.* New York: MacMillan.

Zilboorg, G. (1941). *A history of medical psychology.* New York: Norton.

Selected Bibliography

Almeder, R. (1992). *Death & personal survival: The evidence for life after death.* Lanham, MD: Rowman & Littlefield,

Baruss, I. (1990). *The personal nature of notions of consciousness: A theoretical and empirical examination of the role of the personal in the understanding of consciousness.* Landham, MD: University Press of America.

Bucke, R.M. (1923). *Cosmic consciousness* (2nd ed.). New York: E.P. Dutton.

Bullis, R.K. (1992). Psychotherapists and the mystical process. *Journal of Contemporary Psychotherapy, 22,* 43-49.

Dillbeck, M.C. (1983). The Vedic psychology of the Bhagavad-Gita. *Psychologia, 26,* 62-72.

Ellwood, R.S. (1993). *Islands of the dawn: The story of alternative spirituality in New Zealand.* Honolulu, HI: University of Hawaii Press.

Feldman, J., & Rust, J. (1989). Religiosity, schizotypal thinking, and schizophrenia. *Psychological Reports, 65,* 587-593.

Foster, G.W. (1985). *The world was flooded with light: A mystical experience remembered.* Pittsburgh, PA: University of Pittsburgh Press.

Frankl, V. (1975). *The unconscious God: Psychotherapy and theology.* New York: Simon & Schuster.

Goldberg, B. (1982). *Past lives, future lives.* New York: Ballantine.

Grof, S., & Grof, C. (Eds.). (1989). *Spiritual emergency.* New York: Putnam Publishing Group.

Hart, R., & Reed, A.W. (1977). *Maori myth: The supernatural world of the Maori.* Wellington, NZ: A.H. & A.W. Reed, Ltd.

Hauser, S.T., Vieyra, A.B., Jacobson, A.M., & Wertlieb, D. (1989). Family aspects of vulnerability and resilience in adolescence: A theoretical perspective. In T.F. Dugan & R. Coles (Eds.), *The child In our times: Studies in the development of resiliency* (pp. 109-131). New York: Brunner/Mazel.

Heath, D.H. (1983). The maturing person. In R. Walsh & D. H. Shapiro (Eds.), *Beyond health and normality: Explorations of exceptional well-being* (pp. 52-206). New York: Van Nostrand Reinhold.

Koestler, A (1973). *The roots of coincidence.* New York: Vantage Books.

Kuhn, T.S. 1977). *The essential tension: Selected studies in scientific tradition and change.* Chicago: University of Chicago Press.

Laing, R.D. (1987). Hatred of health. *Journal of Contemplative Psychotherapy, 4,* 77-86.

Lajoie, D.H., & Shapiro, S.I. (1992). Definitions of transpersonal psychology: The first twenty-three years. *Journal of Transpersonal Psychology, 24,* 79-98.

Lukoff, D. (1985). The diagnosis of mystical experiences with psychotic features. *Journal of Transpersonal Psychology, 17,* 155-181.

Lukoff, D., & Lu, F. (1988). Transpersonal psychology research review topic: Mystical experience. *Journal of Transpersonal Psychology, 20,* 161-184.

Lukoff, D., Lu, F., & Turner, R. (1992). Toward a more culturally sensitive DSM-IV. *The Journal of Nervous and Mental Disease, 180,* 673-682.

Lukoff, D., Turner, R., & Lu, F. (1992). Transpersonal psychology research review: Psychoreligious dimensions of healing. *Journal of Transpersonal Psychology, 24,* 41-61.

Lusseyran, J. (1963). *And there was light* (E. Cameron, trans.). Boston: Little, Brown.

Maslow, A.H (1969). Various meanings of transcendence. *Journal of Transpersonal Psychology, 1,* 56-66.

Maslow, A.H. (1972). *The farther reaches of human nature.* New York: Penguin Books.

Metzner, R. (1980). Ten classical metaphors of self-transformation. *Journal of Transpersonal Psychology, 12,* 47-62.

Montgomery, C.L. (1991). The care-giving relationship: Paradoxical and transcendent aspects. *Journal of Transpersonal Psychology, 23,* 91-105.

Moody, R. (1975). *Life after life: The investigation of a phenomenon—survival of bodily death.* New York: Bantam Books.

Moss, T. (1974). *The probability of the impossible.* New York: New American Library.

Paulsell, W.O. (1989). William James and Bernard of Clairvaux on mystical experience. *Studies in Formative Spirituality, 10,* 171-180.

Pollner, M. (1989). Divine relations, social relations, and well-being. *Journal of Health and Social Behavior, 30,* 92-104.

Roberts, J. (1974). *The nature of personal reality: A Seth book.* Englewood Cliffs, NJ: Prentice-Hall.

Rogers, C.R. (1963). The concept of the fully functioning person. *Psychotherapy Research, Theory, and Practice, 1,* 17-26.

Rosen, G. (1968). *Madness in society: Chapters in the historical sociology of mental illness.* New York: Harper & Row.

Seeman, J. (1983). *Personality integration.* New York: Human Science Press.

Smith, J.C. (1975). Meditation as psychotherapy: A review of the literature. *Psychological Bulletin, 88,* 558-564.

Steinmetz, P. (1984). *Meditations with Native Americans—Lakota spirituality.* Santa Fe, NM: Bear & Company.

Schwarzbaum, H. (1989). *Jewish folklore between East and West.* Beer-Sheva, Israel: Ben-Gurion University of the Negev Press.

Swinomish Tribal Mental Health Project. (1991). *A gathering of wisdoms: Tribal mental health: A cultural perspective.* Mount Vernon, WA: Swinomish Tribal Community.

Underhill, E. (1915). *Practical mysticism.* New York: E.P. Dutton.

Vaughan, F. (1985). Transpersonal vision. *ReVision, 8,* 11-15.

Vaughan, F. (1991). Spiritual issues in psychotherapy. *Journal of Transpersonal Psychology, 23,* 105-119.

Walsh, R., & Shapiro, D.J., Jr. (Eds.). (1983). *Beyond health and normality: Explorations of exceptional psychological well-being.* New York: Van Nostrand Reinhold.

Washburn, M. (1990). Two patterns of transcendence. *Journal of Humanistic Psychology, 30,* 84-112.

Weis, B.L. (1988). *Many lives, many masters.* New York: Simon and Schuster.

White, J. (Ed.). (1984). *What Is enlightenment: Exploring the goal of the spiritual path.* Los Angeles: Jeremy P. Tarcher.

White, R. (Ed.). (1976). *Surveys in parapsychology: Reviews of the literature with updated bibliographies.* Metuchen, NJ: Scarecrow Press.

Wolff-Salin, M. (1986). *No other light: Points of convergence in psychology and spirituality.* New York: Crossroad.

Author Index

Subject Index